SEA BOAT FISHING

A MANUAL FOR BEGINNERS

By the same author

Escape to Sea
Fishing Boats and Equipment
Fishing Gear and Methods
Fishing Questions and Answers
Leaves from my Logbook

SEA BOAT FISHING

A Manual For Beginners

JOHN BURGESS

THE BOYDELL PRESS

First published 1988 by The Boydell Press
an imprint of Boydell & Brewer Ltd
PO Box 9, Woodbridge, Suffolk IP12 3DF

ISBN 0 85115 494 8

British Library Cataloguing in Publication Data

Burgess, John, *1911–*
Sea boat fishing : a manual for beginners.
1. Saltwater fishing
I. Title
799.1'6 SH457

ISBN 0–85115–494–8

Printed and bound in Great Britain by
the Camelot Press Ltd, Southampton

CONTENTS

ILLUSTRATIONS

Foreword

I have a friend who, when he retired, bought a small stoutly-built boat which he uses for fishing. He proceeds to sea, whenever weather and circumstances permit, and returns with soles, shrimps and other species with which to regale his family and friends. He has told me that, by so doing, a whole new world of interest has been opened to him. He is full of enthusiasm about his activities and always has some instructive and/or amusing information to impart about them. I know a score of characters approaching his age who have retired or been made redundant and apparently have nothing better to do than hang about their clubs or exercise their wives' poodles. They are far from enthusiastic about anything. There must be thousands of their kind in coastal areas who do not appreciate the fact that the sea is a vast self-replenishing store of fresh food from which they can help themselves at will and derive health and enjoyment by doing so. There must be as many, or more, young men who are unable to obtain employment and do not appreciate the fact either. There may, however, be many who do not regard the sea as little else than 'miles and miles of bloody wet' and who would like to fish for the pot in their spare time if they knew how to do so. Should you be one of them, this manual is for you. It contains basic information which will enable you to fish with simple gear which does not require any special skills to operate – gear which can be worked from any small open or half-decked boat. You don't need an expensive boat, fitted with all sorts of modern gadgets, to catch fish at sea. If you are young and impecunious, you can work lines, hoop nets, gill and tangle nets, and a few shellfish traps from a small rowing boat. If you are not so young and have modest funds at your disposal, you can work a larger open boat – equipped perhaps with sails and/or an outboard engine – to fish further afield. And, if you are comparatively well-off when you retire, you will be able to afford a 20–30 ft boat equipped both with sails and an inboard engine, and fitted with a cabin to enable you to camp on board in comfort. With such a boat you will be able to work a beam trawl in addition to the other types of gear mentioned.

You may wish to know what my qualifications are for offering this information. After handlining for snapper and flathead, trolling for tuna and barracouta, and lobstering from Twofold Bay in Australia for several years, I engaged in big game and other fishing from Sydney, New South Wales, for several more. Having to return to the UK for domestic reasons, I started to write for *Fishing News* and eventually contributed a column to the journal every week for twenty years. During that time I operated a boat for the purpose of testing new equipment, fishing gear and methods. In it I engaged in handlining and trolling; longlining; trammel netting; drift, gill and ray netting; eel trapping; shellfish trapping; and beam and otter trawling.

Information in the first section of the manual is, therefore, derived from first hand experience. Information in the second section has been gleaned from perusal of works in the library at the Fisheries Laboratory, Lowestoft, and interrogation of helpful scientists there. That in the third consists of answers which I had to ferret out in order to reply to questions received from readers of *Fishing News*. In the Glossary are a selection of words and phrases, the meanings of which I have been doubtful about at one stage or another.

I hope the manual will serve not only to help you catch all the fish you want for the pot but to increase your knowledge of the sea and its bounty.

John Burgess died on 2 December, 1987, before *Sea Boat Fishing* was published.

CHAPTER ONE

Methods

1. HANDLINING AND TROLLING

Gear

Gear required for handlining comprises lines, reels, swivels, hooks, sinkers, lures and/or bait, gaff and/or landing net. A large wooden fid, leaded at the blunt end, is a useful weapon to have as well; its weighted end can be used to dispatch obstreperous fish and its pointed end to compel disgorgement of hooks.

Cotton and hemp lines used to be used but in recent years there has been a trend towards increased use of lines made from synthetic twines as they are stronger, size for size, and will not rot even if stowed wet. Twisted polyethylene, spun nylon, braided polyester (Terylene) lines, attached by swivel to a trace or cast made of monofilament nylon are among the most popular. All you need by way of a reel is a square wooden frame.

Swivels need to be large enough to take the main line and to be well lubricated if they are to be effective. One between the main line and trace, and another between the latter and the line joining it to the sinker, is a satisfactory arrangement. The latter line and the trace are customarily of lesser breaking strength than the main line so that in the case of hooks and/or sinker becoming fouled, none of the main line is lost.

For catching mackerel from an anchored or drifting boat, feathered lures on 1/0 hooks are generally used. Casts of up to twenty hooks are attached about 305 mm apart to monofilament nylon by 76 mm droppers made from the same size and type of line. Feathers are generally the best artificial lure for mackerel all round the coast of the UK. On heavier casts they are also used to take cod and codling around the coast of Scotland.

More popular for taking cod in Scottish waters, though, is a unique type of ripping gear. It consists basically of a one hundred metre main line with a breaking strength of over 45 kg, a lead 'boom', two metres of line with a breaking strength of under 45 kg and a lead 'fish' with four rubber eels attached to it.

Rubber eels of all sorts of colours and sizes are used for ripping. A popular arrangement is to attach to the lead fish a white one on a 9/0 hook, a red one on a 7/0 hook, a black one on a 7/0 hook and a yellow one on a 5/0 hook.

Feathers and artificial eels or worms are likely to be effective when the water is clear enough for fish to see them. When it is not, as is usually the case on shallow, sandy parts of the British coast, some form of bait will prove more attractive.

Baits

Fresh is usually preferable to salted bait for catching mackerel and they are particularly partial to whitebait, sand eels and small sprats. But it is unnecessary to go to much trouble to procure these as you can usually catch one or two with a bit of bacon to start with and then cut 'lasks' from their bellies and re-bait with them. They will take these voraciously and when you have boated a few, you will have all the fresh bait you want.

Cod will usually take mussels, lugworms, squid, sprats, herring or soft crabs with enthusiasm. And they will sometimes take any form of fish bait, fresh or salted. They are not as particular as some species about their diet and a list of the unusual objects that have been found among the contents of their stomachs is amazing.

Not only are lugworms relished by most species you are likely to catch but they are readily available in many places. On beaches and mudbanks where there are plenty of worm casts, you can dig up an adequate supply of them in a short time if you use a broad-tined fork.

In theory you will see a dimple in the sand or mud about 230 mm away from each cast. If you sink the fork about 50 mm into such a dimple and rock it backwards and forwards, water will start to bubble from the cast, or from another close to it. This indicates that a worm is lying head towards the dimple in a U-shaped tunnel between that cast and the dimple. If you then remove a forkful from the dimple end of the tunnel and, if necessary, dredge towards the cast, you are likely to capture the worm.

In practice you may not be able to see water bubbling from either the cast you think it is going to or from any in its close vicinity; as often as not in this country rain is pouring down when you are digging lugworms. But if you work on this principle and dredge deeply and swiftly between dimples and nearby casts, you will soon collect all the worms you want.

Lugworms are the most favoured of all baits for taking most species with handlines. They are relished by cod, haddock, pollack, coalfish, soles, plaice and dabs. They are most attractive when freshly dug but they can be

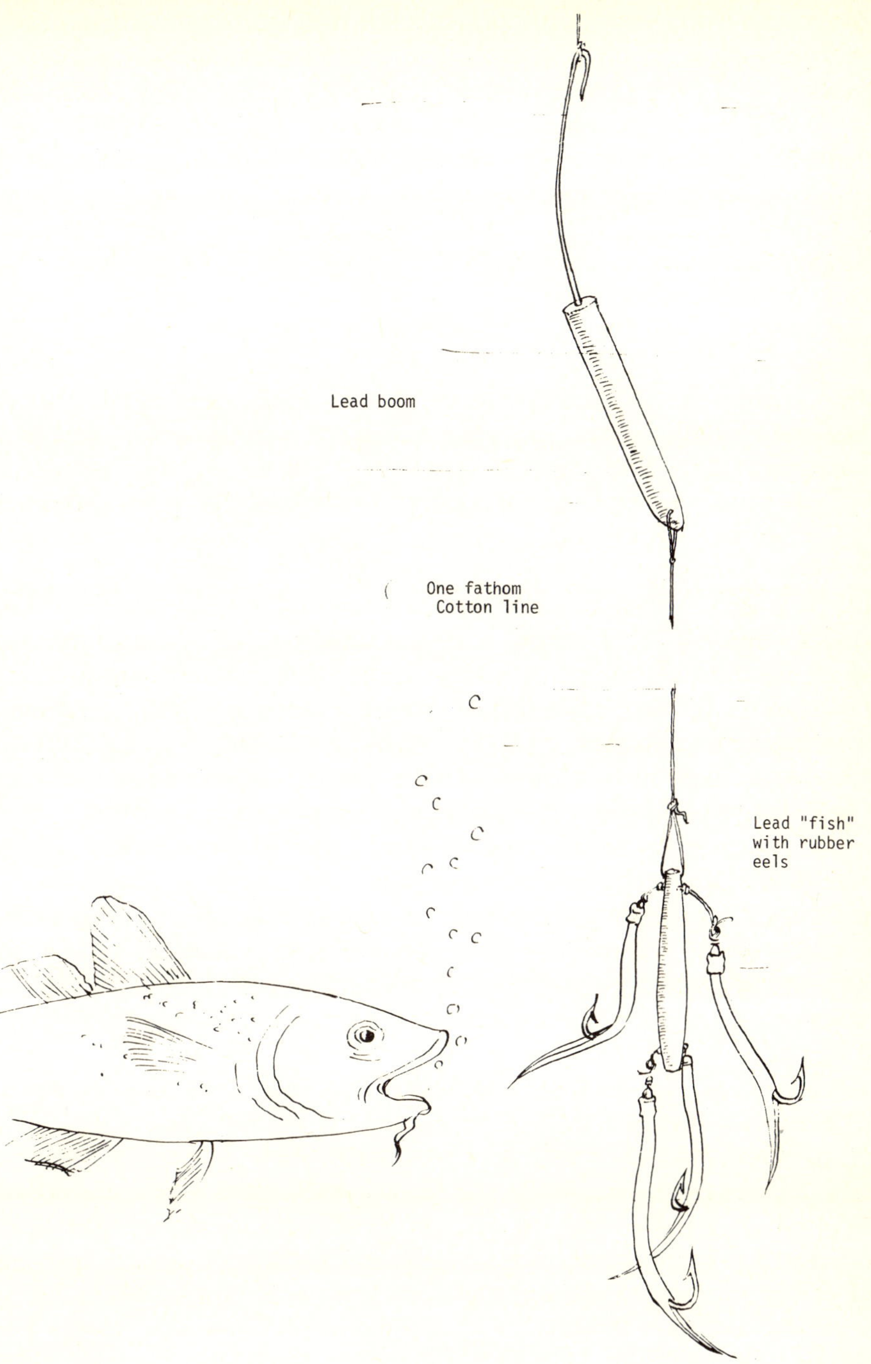

Cod ripping gear

preserved in various ways and still retain much of their attraction.

Following closely on their heels (if any!) as attractive baits come pieces of fresh herring, mackerel, pilchards and sprats. The flesh of these fish is oily and leaches attractive juices. All cod-like species relish these baits and so do conger eels and dogfish. If used as live bait, sand eels are highly attractive to bass, turbot, red gurnard and John Dory.

Soft crabs are another type of bait attractive to all cod-like species. They are also relished as much by skates and rays as are hermit crabs. Prawns and shrimps are not infrequently used as bait. They are attractive to most species, especially flat fish, but are not used as extensively as mussels. The latter soon get washed off hooks but whelks and pieces of squid – equally attractive baits – don't. Pieces of squid are particularly attractive to conger eels and halibut although the latter are generally taken on hooks baited with small codling, coalfish or whiting.

To rig lines

If you are going to fish for cod, codling, whiting and any other species which may take the hook while doing so, an effective way to rig your line is to attach about four metres of 30 kg breaking strength monofilament nylon to the business end of your main line by means of a swivel in good condition.

Having done so, you make two loops in the nylon about 305 mm and 1.5 m from the lower end; then attach a sinker by 305 mm of line with a breaking strength of 12 kg. The loops (about 203 mm long) serve as droppers and the outer ends of them can be attached easily and speedily to ringed hooks.

Fitted in this way, the hooks can be replaced quickly too. If, say, you start fishing with 5/0 hooks and then find that there are plenty of small codling and whiting about but few fish of any size, you can substitute 2/0 hooks without wasting time.

Hooks and sinkers

A word or two about hooks might be of use to you at this stage. Two factors affect the size of a hook: its pattern and the width of its gap (distance between point and shank). Hook sizes of different patterns, therefore, vary to some extent and the only way to define them precisely is to quote both quality and size number together.

Most hook manufacturers conform to the general practice of categorising a hook measuring about 11 mm across the gap as a Size One hook, those above that size as 1/0 to 10/0 etc. and those below it as 2 to 20 etc. but consistency in this respect is far from universal. And even individual manufacturers

Manually operated reels are useful for capturing cod in deep water

5

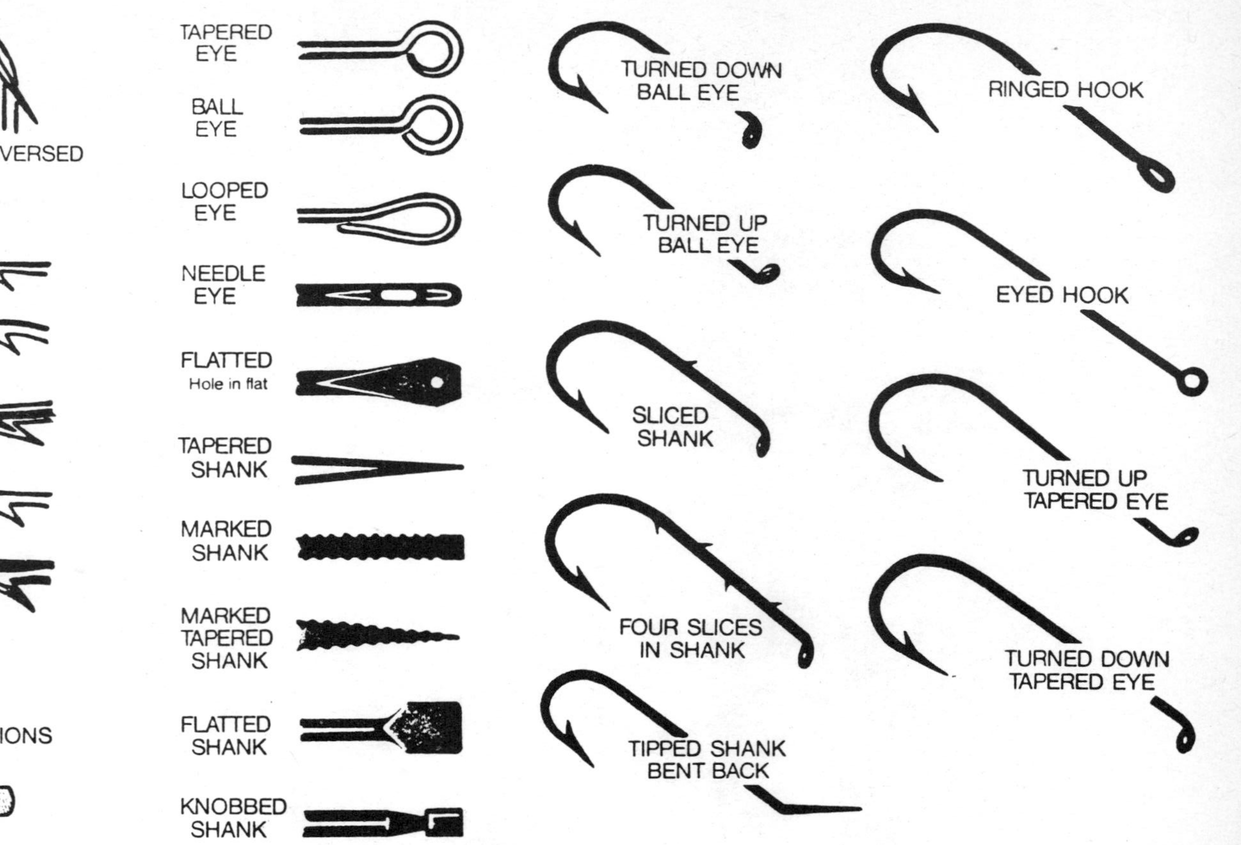
KIRBED
STRAIGHT
REVERSED
HOLLOW POINT
CURVED IN POINT
SUPERIOR POINT
DUBLIN POINT
KNIFE EDGE POINT
SHANK CROSS SECTIONS
REGULAR
FORGED
TAPERED EYE
BALL EYE
LOOPED EYE
NEEDLE EYE
FLATTED Hole in flat
TAPERED SHANK
MARKED SHANK
MARKED TAPERED SHANK
FLATTED SHANK
KNOBBED SHANK
TURNED DOWN BALL EYE
TURNED UP BALL EYE
SLICED SHANK
FOUR SLICES IN SHANK
TIPPED SHANK BENT BACK
RINGED HOOK
EYED HOOK
TURNED UP TAPERED EYE
TURNED DOWN TAPERED EYE

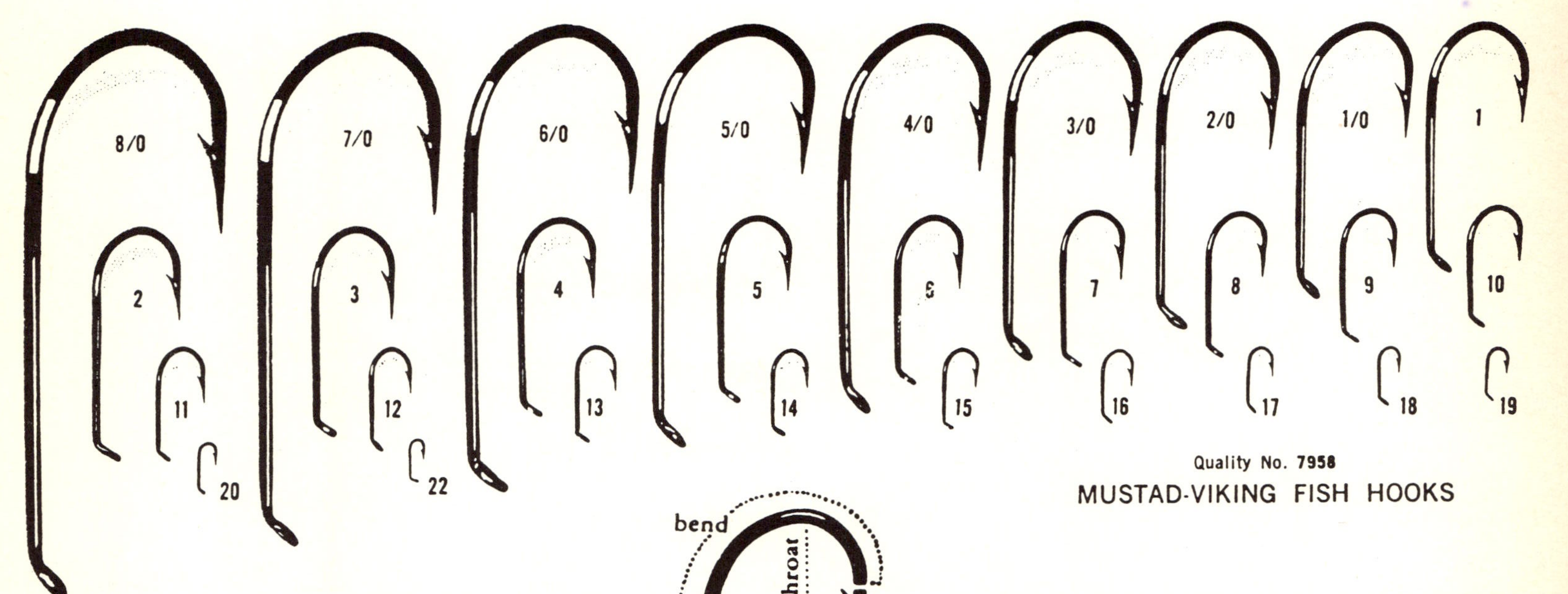

Quality No. 7958
MUSTAD-VIKING FISH HOOKS

The size of a fish hook is determined by its pattern; it is given in terms of the width of the gap of the hook. An example: the illustration above shows Mustad-Viking fish hooks, quality No. 7958, all actual sizes and with correct size numbers. All hooks of Mustad-Viking pattern conform to these sizes.

The hook sizes of other patterns are bound to differ to some extent; the quality number and size number of a hook should therefore always be quoted together, and regarded as inseparable.

Mustad hook terminology

On the illustration at the left, the various parts of a fish hook are shown together with their names. The two important dimensions of the hook are made clear: its gap and its throat. The hook shown here is a Mustad-Viking hook. Note the width of the gap, the clearance between point and shank, and the depth of the throat of the hook. These generous dimensions make for a bigger bite, for deeper penetration of the point, and for better holding power. The weight of the fish is carried high up on the centre of the bend.

sometimes describe the sizes of their hooks in different ways.

It is impossible to say which is the best size and type of hook for catching any particular species as preference varies from place to place and from year to year. But manufacturers provide a useful clue when they offer haddock, halibut, conger hooks etc. You can be sure that the latter will not only be suitable for catching conger but for catching skates, rays and dogfish as well.

In normal circumstances a conical lead sinker weighing about a kilo is adequate for handlining mackerel. But when they are really 'on the bite' a 2kg sinker makes it easier to remove them from trace or cast. It helps to prevent heavy fish from swiming around each other and other parts of the cast in the first place and it keeps the cast vertical in the water when you have hauled it to the surface and commenced to remove the fish from it.

Several mackerel on a line with a light sinker can snarl a cast so much that you will be tempted to lift it on board with the fish still on the hooks. Once you have done so, they will tangle it still more and you may lose valuable fishing time.

Removing mackerel from hooks presents no problems but, if a cod or comparatively large fish swallows a hook, you will probably need your fid to remove it. Hold the fish up by the trace and dropper, shove the point of the fid well down its throat and then waggle the fid with a circular motion. The hook will come clear.

TROLLING

The word 'handlining' is used to describe line fishing without a rod from an anchored or drifting boat; 'trolling' to describe trailing one or more lines with bait or lures attached from a boat propelled by sail or engine. When the latter method is used for catching mackerel, it is sometimes known as railing or whiffling.

There is no more delightful method of fishing than trolling under sail alone and at times it can be the most effective, too, as there are no propeller noises to scare quarry out of the path of the approaching vessel.

Most items of gear required for trolling – lines, traces, hooks, swivels etc. – are similar to those required for handlining. Additional ones are metal spinners and lures specially designed to be towed by a moving boat; torpedo leads; and, maybe, paravanes for taking lures down deep below the boat or out on either side of it.

Rubber and plastic lures have become as popular, if not more popular, than metal spinners in recent years for taking some species when trolling. A most effective lure for catching bass, for instance, is the Red Gill Sand Eel which is made from a plastic material that becomes opaque and a reddish colour towards gills and head. It has an open snout through which monofilament nylon can be threaded and attached to a 6/0 hook. The point of the hook emerges between the pelvic fins and the tail is left free to waggle and bring the lure to life. Variations of this eel are extensively used for catching cod, pollack and ling around wrecks.

To rig lines

Having equipped yourself with all the gear necessary for trolling, the next job is to rig it.

Since shoals of mackerel may be found feeding on or near the surface, or twenty or more metres below it, it is best to rig one light and one heavy line.

To rig the former, attach a No. 1 swivel to the end of your one hundred metre main line and to the other end of the swivel attach a 230 gm mackerel or spinning lead. To the other end of the lead attach a swivel and four metres of 5 kg breaking strength monofilament nylon. To the end of the nylon attach a mackerel spinner. To rig the latter, carry out the same procedure but substitute a spinning lead weighing a kilo for the 230 gm lead. Wind the lines on 305 mm x 305 mm wooden frames and you are ready for action.

When you leave harbour it will pay you to keep an eye lifting for feeding gulls as they often indicate a shoal of mackerel feeding near the surface. Sometimes gulls will indicate shoals of fish far closer to the harbour entrance than you might have expected and can save you the time that you would have expended in searching if you had not noticed their activities.

Gulls will also, of course, enable you to maintain contact with a shoal once you have located it. And they were, in fact, the principal means of doing so before echo sounders became available for installation in fishing boats. Mackerel move about and may be found anywhere so it is best to proceed to where you expect them to be at no more than 3–4 knots with a couple of lines out.

You will stand a good chance of hooking mackerel from the first shoal you encounter, whether it be on the surface or well below it, if you stream a line with a 230 gm lead and spinner on it from one quarter and a line with a lead weighing a kilo and spinner on it from the other.

You will stand the best possible chance of hooking them if, instead of making the inboard end of the lines fast, each of two men holds one line in his hand and jigs it occasionally. Mackerel, like most other trollable fish, will watch a steadily moving lure before taking or rejecting it. If, however, it darts away from them as natural prey would do, they are likely to pounce on it in case it should escape them altogether.

Fish finders

If you are going to handline and troll for mackerel and many other species, it will help you to do so successfully if you install an echo sounder in which echoes from targets are recorded on paper. Such an instrument is not only a better aid to navigating precisely than one which shows depths by means of a flashing light or meter, but is an invaluable aid to finding fish and fishing grounds.

When faced with the problem of selecting a suitable instrument, you may be in doubt about which transducer frequency it would be best for it to have. In that case the following notes may be of help to you.

Broadly speaking, low frequency sounders are best for finding fish in deep water and high frequency sounders for finding them in shallow water. So that, to go to extremes, if you were proposing exclusively to rip cod in 60–100 metres off the Scottish coast, an instrument with a frequency of about 38 kHz would suit you best and if you were intending to catch mackerel or codling and whiting in less than forty metres, an instrument with a frequency of 143 kHz or over would be the most suitable.

A fact that may well affect your choice is that the higher the frequency of a transducer the smaller it can be made. And since, in small craft, the smaller the transducer the better, your best plan would probably be to opt for an instrument with as high a frequency as will give you the maximum depth range you are likely to require.

If you do install a recording echo sounder, it will be worth remembering that better echoes are received from fish with swim bladders because the latter contain air. Air is a far better reflector than the flesh of a fish and a swim bladder, although only about one twentieth of the size of a fish, accounts for about half the echo.

Cod, whiting, haddock, hake, ling, coalfish, pollack, gurnard, garfish, herring, horse mackerel, grey mullet, pilchards, salmon and sea trout have swim bladders. Turbot only have them when young. Halibut, soles, plaice, dabs, mackerel, dogfish, skates and rays do not have them.

Fishing charts

You will not, I presume, sail forth to capture mackerel or any other species without an up-to-date chart of the area in which you propose to operate. If you are just beginning to fish this will probably be an Admiralty chart providing a wealth of information of value to both navigators and fishermen.

Of even more value to the latter, it could be of interest to you to know, are two series of charts specially produced for fishermen. One is known as the

These echoes from small mackerel (left) and big mackerel were recorded on a Kelvin Hughes Sounder installed in the 30ft Cornish Queen fishing in 45 fathoms off Land's End

Blue Back series and the other as the Kingfisher series.

Blue Back charts cover all coastal areas around the British Isles. They are usually supplied on tough blue manila backing paper. International fishery limit lines as well as submarine cables are shown on most of them. They are all corrected to the date of issue.

Kingfisher charts are large scale fishing charts containing depth contour information and the positions of all known wrecks, cables, pipelines, large boulders and other seabed obstructions. All seabed conditions of interest to fishermen – mud, sand, shingle, rock and coral – are clearly marked on them. They cover all grounds around the British Isles.

2. LONGLINING

Longlining, or set lining, is a method which can be employed for taking many different species of fish. Around the coasts of the British Isles it is principally used for capturing cod, haddock, whiting, saith, ling, skate, dogfish and conger eels.

One of its advantages is that lines can be set on grounds too rough to be trawled as well as on sand and shingle bottom. Another is that it is a flexible method – you can set as much or as little line as you want from practically any size and type of boat. It is therefore eminently suitable for use by beginners.

Gear

All the gear you need to catch enough fish for your own consumption is a line about one hundred metres long, snoods and snood clips, gaff, two fish baskets, a fish box, two small anchors and sufficient lengths of line to attach them to floats in whatever depth of water you are going to fish.

Use of snood clips (above) and snap-on connectors simplifies operations when longlining

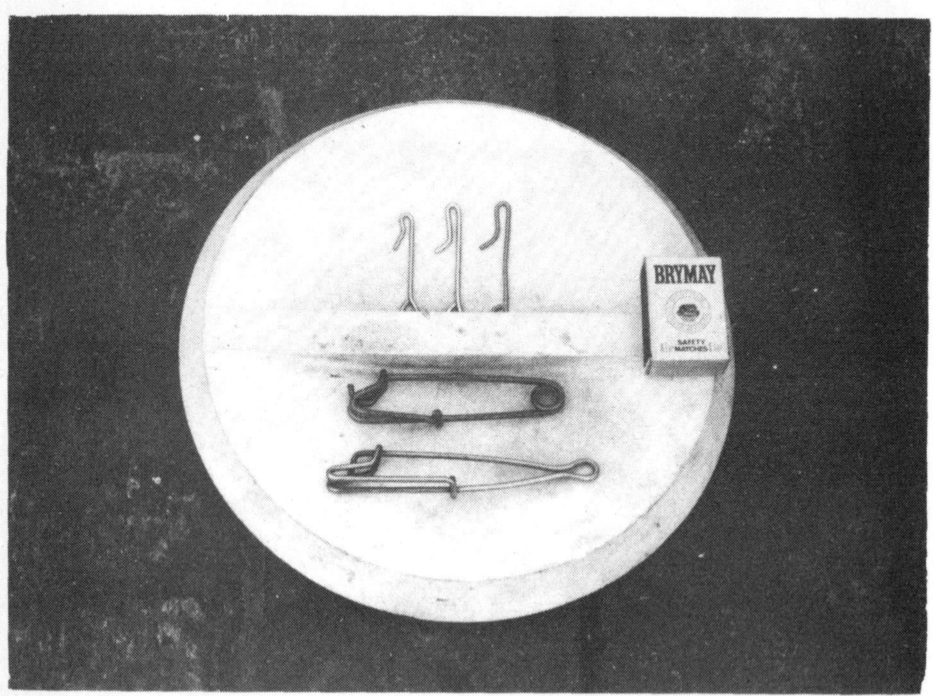

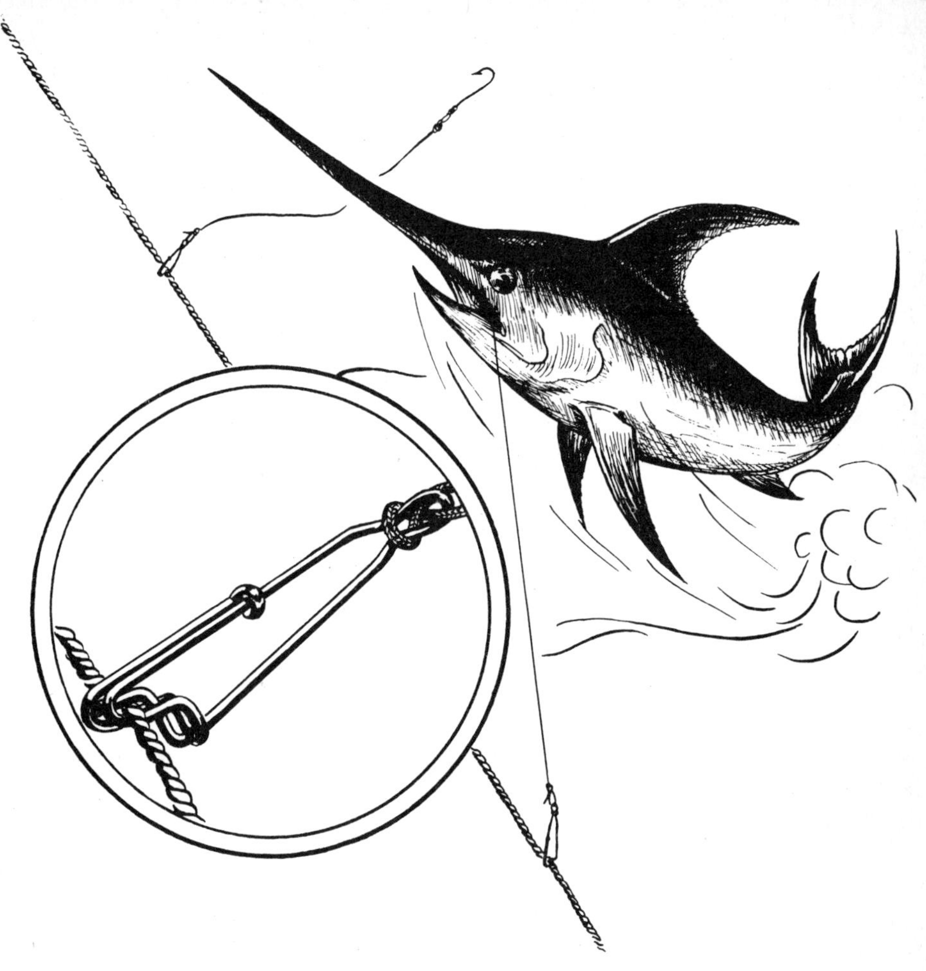

Snap-on connectors are useful not only when longlining for swordfish but for smaller species

Spun nylon or twisted polyester (Terylene) lines are likely to prove most satisfactory as they are easy to handle and do not rot when stowed wet. Line about 2 mm in diameter with a breaking strength of about 90 kg is likely to prove adequate.

Snoods 610–760 mm long made of either monofilament nylon, twisted or braided Terylene are likely to prove satisfactory unless the ground on which you set your lines is infested with crabs. In that case snoods made of twisted or braided polythene are likely to give better results because polythene floats and such snoods will tend to lift baited hooks off the bottom out of the way of the crabs.

I think you will definitely find it best in the long run to attach snoods to line with clips (snap-on connectors) instead of knots. If they are attached by knots, you have to be highly skilled to shoot and haul them without their getting tangled. Speed of shooting and hauling is not a vital factor in your case and clips enable you to attach snoods as your boat drifts and to remove them as you haul. Should line and snoods ever get badly snarled, they will be far easier to clear if you can separate them.

Flatted or Spade hooks are generally used by professional longline fishermen because if they use ringed hooks and are setting lines at high speed, there is always a chance of the point of one hook getting through the ring of another and causing an almighty snarl-up. But I think you would be better off with ringed hooks because they are easier to attach to, and detach from, snoods. I also think that you would be better off with nickel alloy rather than tinned hooks as the former will not rust.

I think you will find that plastic fish baskets are preferable to wicker ones for your purposes as lines coiled down in them do not get snagged by protruding pieces of wicker. An ordinary wooden fish box is adequate for the ready use stowage of baited hooks and the snoods and clips attached to them.

Two small Bruce anchors will probably prove better than any other type for holding your line in position when you have set it. Weight for weight the holding power of this type of anchor is greater than that of most other types – on all kinds of bottom – and they are easy to handle. Small diameter spun polypropylene line is probably best for attaching them to floats. The latter should be brightly coloured and not more than about 200 mm in diameter. If you use large floats or buffs for marking the end of your line, it's odds on that some Charlie will pick one of them up, thinking it's a mooring buoy.

Rigging and baiting

Whatever type of line you buy, it will pay you to stretch it thoroughly by towing it astern of your boat before attaching snoods to it. A line so stretched will coil down in a basket without kinking and will be far easier to handle when baiting and shooting.

To attach snoods to ringed hooks, first pass the bight of the snood from back to front through the ring; make a half hitch round the shank and then pass the bight of the snood over the point of the hook; draw the knot tight and then slide it down the shank to the back of the ring. To attach snoods to clips presents no problem.

How far apart you attach snoods to the line while it is running out from the basket over the gunwhale depends on what species of fish you are after.

When setting lines for small fish such as whiting, some liners attach them about 1.4 m apart; when setting them for cod and skate, about 2.8 m apart. As a rule two metres apart is as satisfactory a distance as any if you are using 610 mm snoods.

The same types of bait are used for longlining as for handlining and whatever type you use, the same applies: it should be as fresh as possible. A letter which I once received from a fisherman in Northern Ireland emphasises this point.

He was working 1200 hooks for dogfish in the vicinity of Dundalk Bay when he wrote: 'We use fresh herring for bait. If we do not get out, because of the weather, on the day following the baiting, it is useless to shoot the lines. All the baits just come in again untouched'.

If you have no local knowledge about the best places to shoot your line, you will probably get the best results if you set it along the edges of rough ground.

Examination of a fishing chart of your area, or of an Admiralty chart, will enable you to determine the position of such ground. On fishing charts patches of rough are usually specially drawn and on Admiralty charts they may be marked with an 'R' meaning rock, 'St.' – stones, 'P' – pebbles and 'G' – gravel.

Grounds

On the chart you can lay off bearings of shore marks or light vessels which will enable you to find your way to whatever patch of rough you want to try. And, when you are in the approximate position of it, you can use your echo sounder and/or your leadline to determine its limits.

Even the smallest echo sounder will indicate rocky bottom. The trace on the recorder paper, instead of appearing as a straight line as it does when echoes are being received from sand, shingle or mud bottom, appears as a much rougher marking that leaves you in no doubt about the nature of the seabed.

If the patch of rough ground which you are in search of consists of stones, pebbles or gravel, you may be able to find it with your sounder. You will certainly be able to do so with your lead.

If you arm the hole in the bottom of the lead with tallow or thick grease and start sounding as soon as you think you are approaching the edge of it, you will soon begin to pick up gravel or small stones in the grease. Or you may cease to get sand or mud on it and see nothing but small indentations in it.

In either case, you will know that you are running off on to rough bottom and are, in fact, just about in the position you want to set your line.

Shooting and hauling

Careful preparation and considerable skill are required to shoot a typical longline – say ten one hundred metre lines with 400–500 hooks on them – in coastal waters. But setting a single one hundred metre line at slow speed, attaching snoods to it by means of clips as it runs out, is a comparatively simple operation which you can carry out either from your boat or your dinghy. Sometimes direction of wind and tidal current are such that you can shoot the line while drifting. If not, you can motor or row at slow speed to ensure that it is set where you want it.

Depending on the size of your boat – and weather conditions, of course – I think you will generally find it best to use your dinghy for hauling the line. First thing to do is to recover the float at the leeward end of the line and then its anchor. After they are inboard, you can start hauling, removing snood clips as you do so. Normally you will probably find it best to shake fish off the hooks into the bottom of the boat and replace snoods etc. in the fish box.

One advantage of using the dinghy for hauling is that, when you have recovered the line and the anchor and float at the other end of it, you can then either row ashore to clean the catch or leave both gear and catch in the dinghy until you can do so. In this way none but cleaned fish are brought onboard the boat in a basket, too late for them to flap about and cover interior surfaces with scales. An additional advantage is that the dinghy can be cleaned thoroughly while on the beach.

Alternative methods

It is the practice of a man I know who lives by the shore of a vast, sheltered bay, prolific with fish, to lay a couple of longlines about the beginning of June and to leave them set until the beginning of September.

He attaches forty snoods and 6/0 hooks to each line about two metres apart, leaving a few metres of the outer ends bare of snoods, and lays the lines out in the middle of the bay on sand and gravel bottom with a 30kg weight at either end to keep them in position.

He secures small lifting lines with floats on them close to the first hook at either end of the lines so that he can lift the latter and under run them without having to lift the weights. And he goes off in his boat once or twice a day, as circumstances dictate, to haul and re-bait the lines.

It is an easy and moderately rewarding method of longlining but its employment depends on your living on the spot and having the time to attend to your lines at least once a day.

If a beach is easily accessible to you and you have not got a boat, you can usually catch a few fish for the table in most places by laying lines along it at low water. From some you can dig cockles and bait your hooks with them; in the close vicinity of others mussels and soft crabs may be readily available for bait.

Should you employ this method, you are likely to find it advisable to cover your baits with sand after you have laid your lines; otherwise you may catch more gulls than fish.

Best length of time to leave your line down will be determined by a number of factors. If sharks, seals and other predators are likely to help themselves to fish hooked on it, your catch will be greatest if you set it about an hour after low water and haul it when the tide begins to slacken about an hour before high water.

If you are using soft baits such as mussels, it will probably pay you to do likewise. So it will if the weather is deteriorating and you might not be able to recover it if you leave it down overnight. Otherwise best practice is likely to be to set it at slack water one day and haul it at slack water the next.

3. GILL AND TANGLE NETTING

Gill netting

Until a few years ago the most commonly used type of gill net used in British waters was a small meshed net used to capture herring, mackerel, pilchards and sprats. As it was not fixed to the seabed but was attached to a boat or a series of buoys and remained free to move with wind and/or tide, it came to be known as a Drift Net.

This type of net has been defined as 'a wall of netting suspended in the sea with a mesh of such a size that the species of fish being sought will swim part way through and then be meshed by its gills'. It is still used extensively by small craft in coastal waters but has been superseded by pelagic trawls and purse seine nets for use in offshore fishing vessels.

Drift netting is a selective method of fishing. Immature fish, too small to become enmeshed, escape undamaged and live to grow to marketable size. It is therefore a highly suitable method to use from a conservation point of view.

So, too, is the use of gill nets of larger mesh size to capture salmon, sea trout, bass, cod and cod-like species, mullet etc. if too much havoc is not wrought in a fishery by using lethal monofilament nylon nets.

Both drift and gill netting are passive methods of fishing. You wait for the fish to swim into your nets instead of engulfing or encircling them. Employment of them does not necessarily require the use of engines and deck machinery and they can therefore be commended to beginners.

Until about 1950 drift nets always used to be made of cotton treated with cutch, alum, linseed oil and/or tar to stiffen and preserve them. Since then multifilament or staple spun nylon nets have become increasingly popular as they are very strong, will not rot and do not have to be repeatedly cutched.

Nylon is undoubtedly the most suitable synthetic twine for making them as it has a comparatively high specific gravity and will sink in sea water. Nets made from it will sink and take up a nearly vertical position when suspended from a floatline.

The size of coastal drift nets varies from about 20–80 metres long and 4–6 metres deep. They are set in by the half – one hundred metres of unstretched netting on fifty metres of floatline, for example – or in other proportions such as a third or a quarter. Their exact length is usually defined in rows; their mesh size in rows per metre; and their depth in score of meshes.

A mesh size of 25–29 rows per metre is generally accepted as being the most suitable for gilling mackerel; 29–35 for large herring; 36 for small herring; 36–38 for pilchards; and 62–66 for sprats.

Nylon drift nets are made of the same sized twine throughout and are attached directly to headlines. The latter are made up of two ropes, with their lay in opposite directions, joined together. At intervals of about a metre the headlines have plastic floats, instead of the corks traditionally used, attached.

Gill nets nowadays are invariably made of nylon – either multifilament, monofilament or multi-monofilament. They are usually made of about 120 metres of sheet netting rigged to sixty metres long by 3–5 metres deep for fishing.

Mesh sizes available vary from 76 mm (38 mm bar) to 230 mm (115 mm bar). 76 mm mesh is usually used for taking small mullet and bass; 102 mm for large mullet and bass, and sea trout; 152–165 mm for salmon; and 178–230 mm for cod and pollack.

There are as many different types of gill nets as there are of drift nets and probably the best way of selecting suitable nets for the areas in which you propose to work either or both of them is to be guided by your supplier. He will know what species you are likely to catch with them on different parts of the coast at different seasons and be able to recommend a suitable net or nets.

Drift nets are, of course, worked only on the surface and all you need to work one is a buoy or two and some lengths of rope. Some gill nets are designed to be worked on the surface and some to be set on the seabed. To work either of them you will need a couple of anchors or lengths of old chain in addition.

Should you have any doubt about whether to get a gill net to work on the surface or one to set on the seabed, I think you will find it preferable to get the former. When at anchor you can moor it where you can keep an eye on the floatline and enjoy the thrill from time to time of seeing several of the floats being drawn below the surface by, perhaps, a sizeable bass in the net. The only time you get a thrill from a net set on the seabed is when you haul it.

Rigging and operating

If you propose to work a drift net, or a gill net designed to float just below the surface, you will doubtless buy it ready rigged. So all you have to do is to attach a float to either end, if you intend to let it drift on its own, or a float at one end and 10–20 metres of rope at the other if you intend to lie leeward of the net in your boat or dinghy.

Rigging a drift or gill net, therefore, presents no problems. Nor does shooting or hauling either of them. But exactly where and when to shoot them to get the best results requires some knowledge.

As a drift net is comparatively deep, you have to make sure that the depth of water in the direction in which it is likely to drift will be adequate to float it clear of the seabed and of any obstructions. You have to be sure from local knowledge or inquiries that herring, mackerel or whatever your quarry are being taken in the vicinity by professional fishermen. And you have to appreciate that, although mackerel can be taken by daylight, herring are more often taken after dark and most often by moonlight when they rise to the surface.

Although bass and mullet can be caught with gill nets in broad daylight, the best times to use floating gill nets for capturing them are undoubtedly dawn and dusk. Best of all is when it is slack water at these times and there is not much wind.

If, on occasions when working a gill net in the normal way to capture bass and mullet achieves poor results, you might like to work it in an active instead of a passive way. Places to do so are in shallow water near the shore and, if you cruise slowly along it at slack water when there is little wind, you can often detect them by their dorsal fins and disturbed water.

Procedure then is to watch them for a few minutes to determine whether they are feeding and not changing position much or whether they are travelling up or down stream.

If, say, the fish are feeding and are only being carried very slowly upstream by a flood tide, best practice is to land a man with one end of the net to seaward of them and to row round them in a semi-circle. When you have done so and reached the beach, you land with the other end of the net and both of you haul away until the contents of the net are on the beach.

If the fish are travelling up or down stream, it's best to land the man with one end of the net well ahead of them and then tow the net against the current and on to the beach when they have reached a position where they can be encircled.

The process of shooting drift and gill nets presents no problems provided that you have arranged them to run overboard smoothly. Projecting fittings, nuts, bolts and nail heads in some boats, however, are liable to foul the meshes and, if this is the case in your boat, you will find a sheet of canvas measuring about 1½x2 metres can be a useful aid.

If you flake your net down in the middle of it and, before shooting, arrange it so that it covers all fittings likely to foul meshes, operations will proceed smoothly. The canvas will come in handy too if you want to transfer nets from boat to dinghy or vice versa.

Hauling presents few problems provided that, when doing so in a small boat, you don't overload it. A lot of water comes in over the gunwhale together with fish and perhaps weed and, if you don't bale from time to time, you are likely to be in danger of capsizing. If you have to stun obstreperous fish, make sure that you hit their heads and not the boat's planking.

Two or three large and lively bass flapping around among mullet etc. need quietening and can be painful to handle on account of the sharp spines in their dorsal fins. So manoeuvre them on to some netting before you smite them and avoid adding the danger of sinking the boat to that of capsizing it.

A demonstration of what can happen if you wield a bludgeon wildly was given by a character who was longlining between the entrances to the rivers Deben and Ore a year or two ago. He unexpectedly boated a large conger eel and it immediately became a most unruly occupant of his small cockpit. For want of any other weapon to dispatch it, he seized the boat's tiller and aimed a series of blows at it, only succeeding in making it more lively than ever.

Eventually it stopped writhing about for a moment or two and, thinking his chance had come, he aimed an almighty blow at its head. Did he deal it its death blow? He did not. He smashed a hole in the boat's planking and had to make for the shore at top speed with his intended victim writhing about his ankles in rapidly rising water.

Where to work nets

You can soon learn how to rig, shoot and haul drift and gill nets but it takes somewhat longer to learn where to shoot them to achieve satisfactory results. Although there are few alternatives when working drift nets, there are considerably more when working gill nets.

All you have to be sure about when shooting drift nets is that there will be sufficient depth of water and no obstructions in the direction in which they will drift. Then you can shoot them at right angles to the shore at sea or athwart the stream – preferably the flood – in estuaries and rivers.

You can do the same with surface gill nets but you can also moor them in all sorts of different places. You can moor them at right angles to the shore at sea or athwart the stream in estuaries and rivers. But in the latter there are often more productive places to moor them.

Whenever the tidal stream starts to flow at over about a knot, gill nets anchored at both ends tend to become bar taut and to catch more weed and rubbish than fish. So it's better to moor them where they are not affected so much by the current.

In my experience a productive alternative is to anchor them at one end only in the mouths of tributaries to rivers. So positioned they are in line with the main stream and athwart the minor stream, and they do not fill with weed and drag the anchor if left overnight.

Another productive alternative is to moor a net off a point around which there is an eddy. If, about two hours before high water, you fix a stake on the point and then, if necessary, run a nylon line from it to water deep

Little skill is required to shoot and haul a gill net. If you do so in summer, you will seldom fail to catch enough bass and/or mullet for supper

enough for your net, the eddy will assist you to set it athwart the stream.

All you have to do is to shoot it in whatever direction wind, eddy and tide take your boat and then moor the outer end of the net with about 10 kg of old chain. If the tide is still running strongly, it may carry the outer end of the net upstream a bit but the chain will halt it as soon as it slackens.

When the tide turns, it will slowly carry the net in an arc around the point but it will fish athwart the stream for two or three hours. If there is no weed about, you can leave a net set like this for as long as you like, removing fish from it and adjusting the position of the chain from time to time.

Note

According to Dr Andres von Brandt, Professor of Fisheries at Hamburg University, the most important property of a gill net is not to look like an impenetrable wall which fish would avoid. It is essential that it should contrast as little as possible with its surroundings. Dyeing helps a gill net to harmonise with them.

Transparent monofilament gill nets which are scarcely visible and without any disturbing sparkle in the knots have this property more than any other type. And whereas nets dyed blue-green or brown have to be changed over when the colour of the water changes, monofilament nets contrast as little as possible with their surroundings whatever the colour of the water.

Two other factors affect the efficiency of gill nets. It is essential that they are as soft as possible and that the twine from which they are made should not swell when submerged. A swimming fish pushes forward a wave which is reflected by more or less solid objects. The return swell is recorded by a lateral line of the fish which operates as a kind of teleprinter or automatic apparatus for recording distances. The stronger the returning swell, the more the fish will endeavour to avoid what is ahead.

The netting of a gill net should be as fine as possible both for this reason and for the purpose of reducing visibility. To decrease the chances of perception by returning swell, one should not be stretched out rigidly but should be set as slackly as possible.

Tangle netting

The description tangle net is a generic one. It means any kind of net in which fish become entangled instead of being caught by the gills or otherwise entrapped. Customarily, in this country, it means a net consisting of a single wall of netting only, so hung and set in that, when there is no tide running, its bottom half lies loosely on the seabed instead of forming a vertical curtain like the bottom half of a gill net.

In Europe the largest tangle nets of all are worked by Danish fishermen in the North Sea. They are made of 144mm stretched mesh netting and are 70–75 metres long by 6½ meshes deep. Danish practice is to set between 240 and 340 nets in three rows at a distance of about one thousand metres between each two rows. The length of each row is between six and seven thousand metres and every tenth net is secured to a marker buoy which is anchored.

Next largest are ray nets used mostly off the Cornish coast to capture skate, rays and crawfish. They are about 120 metres long set in by the half to fish sixty metres. They are made of very strong nylon twine and are eight meshes (about two metres) deep. Mesh size is about 430mm. Headlines are made of buoyant synthetic ropes without floats on them and footropes are weighted with individual leads. They are worked in fleets with anchors to hold them in position.

Most commonly used tangle nets are trammels which generally consist of Trois Mailles – French for three walls – of netting. Two of them – the outer walls or armouring – are made of large mesh netting and an inner one – the lint or linnett – is made of netting of comparatively small mesh. Fish swim through the large meshes of the outer walls and carry the small mesh inner netting through the large meshes of the outer wall on the other side. Thereafter they are trapped in a pocket from which they seldom escape.

Like other tangle nets, trammels are invariably set on the seabed. They are set to catch demersal fish such as cod, whiting, skate, soles, plaice, bass, mullet etc. but will entangle practically any species. They can be used in fleets or singly and one of such a size that it can be stowed in a single fish basket is a most useful net to have on board as it can be used to catch bait as well as edible fish.

If you want to keep a net on board which will tangle most species and which can be stowed in a single basket, you have the choice of a single or three walled net. And the waters in which you intend to work it mostly will indicate which would serve you best.

If you intend to work it in shallow water mainly for flat fish – water in which there is often a considerable quantity of weed – I think you would be well advised to opt for a single walled net. If you were to get one about fifty metres long by three metres deep, made of fine twisted nylon netting with a mesh size of about 127mm, you would find it comparatively easy to clear of weed, jellyfish etc. Nets of this type have such small floats on the headline that they will fish a little over one metre deep. They have light leadlines attached to the footlines and are very easy to handle.

If you intend to work the net mostly in depths over ten metres where

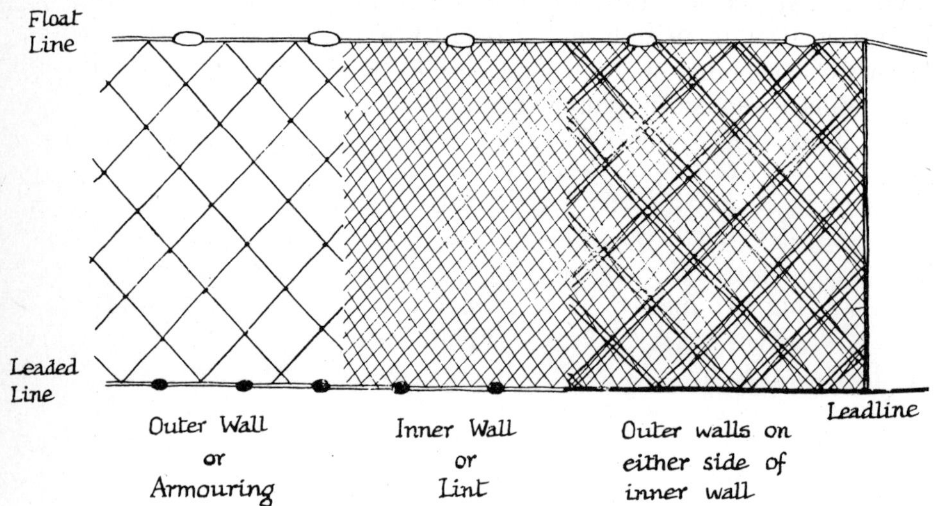

Trammel net

Trammel net mooring

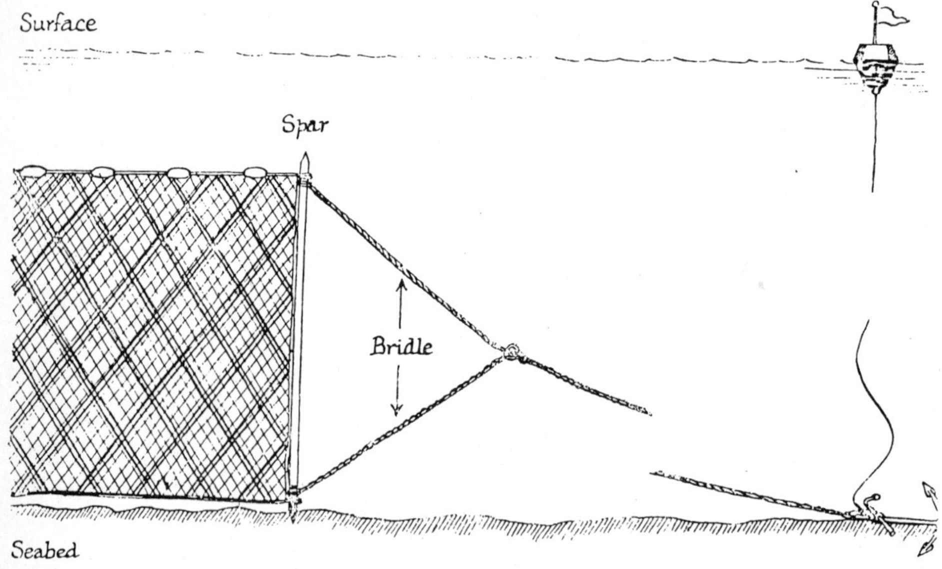

there is little weed, a small trammel net would probably prove the most productive. Such a net is about thirty metres long by one and a half metres deep. It consists of a floatline from which is suspended an inner wall of 76mm or 102mm netting and two outer walls of 457mm mesh netting. Meshes of both inner and outer walls are likely to be hung diamondwise but outer walls are sometimes hung square.

The inner wall of a net of this type is set in by the half – sixty metres of unstretched netting mounted on thirty metres of floatline – and is twice the depth of the outer walls so that it hangs loosely and there is plenty of slack to be carried through the latter. Outer walls are set in by the third unless they are hung square and not set in at all.

Rigging and Operating

Single walled tangle nets and trammels are worked in the same way as gill nets designed to be set on the seabed. To moor one you will need a couple of 7–10kg anchors, anchor ropes and floats or buoys. The lengths of rope you will need depend on where you are going to set the net. If you are going to set in depths over ten metres, you will need at least twenty metres of warp for each anchor; if in shallower water, ten metres will probably suffice.

Three to five times the depth of water in which the net is set is a good guide to the length of anchor buoy lines required. Lines three times the depth will probably suffice where tides do not run at more than two knots. If they run at a greater rate, your marker buoys or floats are less likely to submerge if you use lines five times the depth.

If you are setting a tangle/trammel net in the river, small floats will do as marker buoys. If there is much traffic in the river, you will probably find that it will pay to use brightly coloured ones that have some hope of being seen by clowns careering about without keeping much of a look-out.

One way of rigging the gear of trammels is to fit a 50mm diameter spar, weighted at the bottom end, across each end of the net. But I don't suppose you will want to go to the trouble of doing so as you can make a bridle by joining the end of the floatline to the end of the leadline. If you then bend on the end of the anchor warp about threequarters of the way down this bridle, there will be enough slack in the upper part of it to allow the end of the net to assume a near-vertical position in the water. Attachment of an additional small float at the end of the floatline will help to extend the end of the net vertically.

If you are setting a net in five metres of water or less, you can dispense with any form of bridle. You can attach floats on lines of appropriate length to the ends of the floatline and anchor warps directly to the ends of the leadline.

If you are going to set tangle/trammel nets at sea, undoubtedly the most productive way to work them is to set them at slack water one day and to haul them as the tide slackens the next. If you are going to set one close in to the shore, you will not need much in the way of anchor warps and buoy lines; you can attach an anchor to the end of the footrope itself at the inshore end and a float to the free end of the floatline. You can also attach an anchor to the footrope of the offshore end but you may need a few metres of line for the float at this end if the beach shelves steeply.

When you set a net in this way, you row in to the shore when the speed of the ebb has slackened to about one knot and let go one anchor in about two metres of water. Then one of you rows the boat, heading slightly upstream to counter the effect of the tide, and the other pays the net over the stern so that it is eventually set at right angles to the shoreline.

If you are going to work a net in an estuary or river for bass, mullet etc., you can set it anywhere where it will not be interfered with by other fishermen or passing traffic. In such a position you can set it athwart the stream from about one hour before low water to one and a half to two and a half hours after it. When weed and jellyfish are about, don't leave it down too long as the young flood will soon fill a net with them.

As with gill nets, when setting them in rivers, I have found it rewarding to set tangle/trammel nets across the mouths of tributaries to the mainstream –

Both cod and codling can be caught in a trammel net

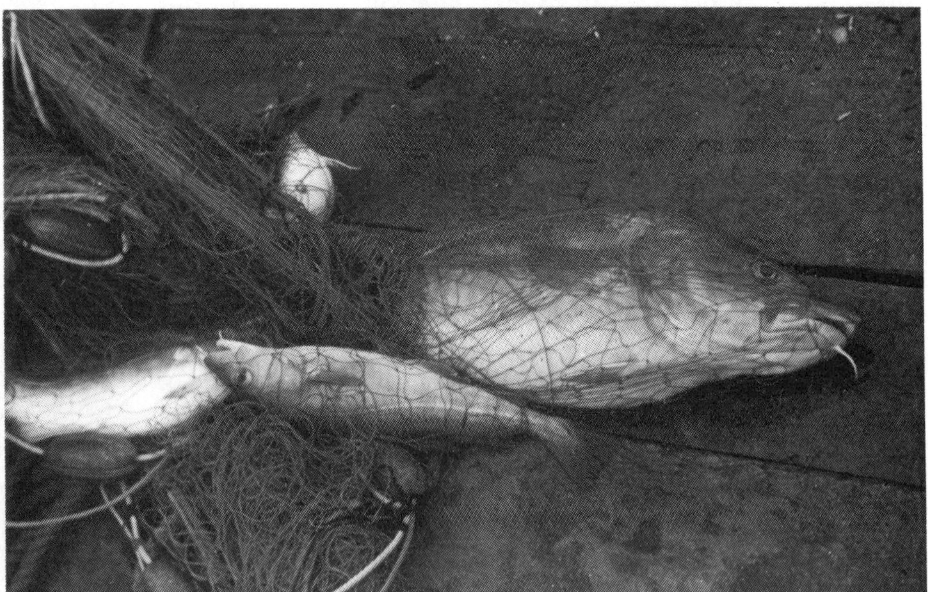

for an hour or two either side of slack water if there is much weed etc. about, all night if there is not.

Notes

Most species of fish are taken in greater quantities in tangle/trammel nets at night than in the daytime. Soles, plaice and other flat fish can be taken when the water is clear; cod and round fish are taken in the greatest quantities when the water is thick and well stirred up. Soles are taken in the greatest quantities on clean, sandy ground used for spawning.

It would appear at first sight to be impossible to to remove some fish from a trammel net without cutting them adrift, so tightly are they enmeshed and wound up in the net. Most, however, can be removed without much difficulty if you open up the mouth of the pocket in which they are trapped. Beware of sharp spines and razor sharp gill covers on some species of fish when removing them.

Lobsters and crabs become entangled in tangle/trammel nets from time to time. The former, surprisingly, can often be extracted without much difficulty. Crabs, on the other hand, are usually extremely difficult or impossible to remove. In the latter case, even if they are edible, the speediest way to deal with them is to smash them into small fragments with a blunt weapon that will not damage the netting. This, of course, is the way to deal with all inedible crabs in a net.

4. SHELLFISH TRAPPING

Shellfish trapping

Capturing shellfish by means of traps is one of the oldest established and most universally used methods of fishing there is. It is employed alike by the most advanced and the most primitive fishermen in the world.

The method, presumably, originated soon after some of our hairy ancestors learnt to make wicker baskets and a bright character among them conceived the idea of baiting a specially designed basket with one of the smaller fish he had speared.

Wicker traps are still used today, in this country and other parts of the world. But there are now probably as many different designs of traps made of materials other than wicker as the number of years that have elapsed since the first trap was set.

They are made of wood, steel, aluminium and plastic materials and covered with synthetic or wire netting of hundreds of different types. They vary in size from huge great cages that can only be hauled by high powered winches installed in ocean-going vessels to those which can easily be hauled by hand from the smallest of boats.

Trapping shellfish is a particularly intriguing form of fishing as you could live for a hundred years and still be discovering more about the habits of your quarry, improved designs for traps, more effective materials with which to make them, and new grounds on which to make captures, every day of your life. Another merit about trapping is that your gear works for you round the clock without requiring constant supervision.

Scientific names for species mentioned in the following pages are:
Lobster – *Homarus vulgaris*
Crawfish – *Palinurus vulgaris*
Crab – *Cancer pagurus*
Dublin Bay Prawn (Norway Lobster) – *Nephrops norvegicus*
Common Prawn – *Leander serratus*
Whelk – *Buccinum undatum*
You will be glad to know that they all taste better than they sound.

Traps and gear

Traps traditionally used around the coast of the British Isles for catching lobsters and crabs can be divided into two principal types – the pot and the creel.

The pot has a single entrance through the top and is mostly used in Cornwall, Devon and along the South Coast of England. The creel has one or two entrances through the sides and is mostly used along the East Coast of England and around the Scottish coast. In Wales and Ireland both types of trap, as well as scores of others, are used.

For trapping crawfish Cornish inkwell pots with large entrances are used exclusively. They are laid to catch lobsters and crabs primarily on grounds which crawfish are known to frequent.

Dublin Bay prawns are mostly caught in steel-framed creels covered with fine mesh netting and fitted with small entrances; Common prawns in miniature pots or creels with several entrances; and whelks in small, heavy steel-framed pots covered with rope instead of netting.

If you have adequate space in your boat to carry fixed frame pots or creels, you will probably make biggest catches with them. If not, you can get folding creels which lie flat when collapsed and which take up little space. One or two of these are likely to prove adequate for catching all the lobsters

Rectangular creel designed and worked successfully for many years by Billy Burrell of Aldeburgh

and crabs you want and, if they are covered in fine mesh netting, all the Dublin Bay prawns you want as well.

Traps for taking Common or Rock prawns take up little space and, if you frequent areas where they are abundant, you are likely to find that it will be rewarding to carry one or two. Though whelk pots are not bulky, they are heavy and I doubt whether you would want to be lumbered with any since you will probably be able to catch all the whelks you want for bait in a hoop net.

A hoop net is easily stowable and a most useful item of gear to have on board. Not only can you catch lobsters and common prawns with one but, if it is made of shrimp netting, whelks and hermit crabs for bait. Incidentally, if you work one while at anchor, you will not infrequently bring up enough shrimps among the other contents to make shrimp sauce.

To work most of these different types of trap, your basic needs will be

Creel – the type of trap used mostly on the East Coast of England and around the coast of Scotland

some form of weight to keep them on the bottom the right way up, lines to lower and haul them with and floats to mark their position.

The purpose of weighting lobster and crab traps that you are going to lay singly is to enable you to place them the right way up precisely where you want on the seabed and to keep them in that position while they are fishing. The minimum weight which will achieve this purpose is, therefore, the one to use; you don't want to have to haul heavier traps than you need.

Weights of between 4 and 7 kg are usually found to be adequate. Should you be using traps made almost entirely of wooden slats, you will probably need all of 7 kg. But if you are using traps made mostly of steel wire or galvanised iron, 4 kg is likely to be all that is required.

Bags of stones, large single stones, slabs of slate, bricks, cement, bits of scrap iron or old chain and iron bars are all used to weight traps. Bricks are not much good as they absorb water and some lobster fishermen are averse to using traps in which there is any iron, either in the frame or by way of additional weight. Cement is popular as it can be poured into a trap so that it becomes attached to the base in the exact position desired. Personally I like parallel strips of bar iron fitted outside of the base of a trap where they will serve to protect as well as weight it.

Traps with bases made of parallel steel slats do not require weighting at all. But all traps with wooden bases do and they need soaking well before you set them for the first time. Until the wood is thoroughly saturated, it will not only tend to float a trap the wrong way up but will release air bubbles likely to make the quarry suspicious and avoid it.

Traps used for catching Dublin Bay prawns do not have to be weighted much, if at all, as they are set on mud and hauled frequently. And not much weight is necessary to keep traps set for the Common prawn in position the right way up. Having perforated iron bases, whelk pots do not need to be weighted at all.

Primary consideration when you come to fitting a float line to a lobster/crab trap is to attach it in such a way that the trap will cause minimum resitance when being hauled and will not revolve or capsize in the process. The usual way to do it is to fit a rope strop to one end of it and to attach the line to it.

So that the line cannot fall across any entrance to the trap at low water, it's best to use floating rope (polyethylene or polypropylene) and attach a float to it at such a distance from the strop that it will watch near the time of low water only. If you then attach two more floats, about four metres apart, to the end of the line at such a distance that they will remain on the surface at high water and in strong tides, you will be able to lift your trap whenever you want.

Baits

When, having weighted and rigged your traps, you get around to baiting them, you are more likely to be concerned with the availability rather than the theoretical desirability of different types of bait.

In theory, lobsters are supposed to prefer stale, and crabs fresh, bait; tough skinned fish like gurnard are preferable to soft species like herring and mackerel as they last longer; fresh or stale bait is preferable to salted bait; the shining silver heads of bass and mullet are more attractive than any kind of fish bait enclosed in a bag of netting; freshly killed cormorants exude oil and are most attractive to lobsters; and large amounts of bait in each trap will ensure greater catches than small amounts. The last is a somewhat dubious theory.

You may know all this about bait but all you may be able to obtain locally are rabbits, bacon bones and tins of pet food. All these will attract lobsters, the latter not only on account of the meat and juices seeping through holes punctured in them but because they shine.

Dublin Bay prawns will take any kind of bait – salt mackerel or herring, conger eel, dogfish etc. They will also go for the bodies of their fellow prawns after the tails have been removed. They do not eat much of the bait and do not tear it to shreds like lobsters and crabs. It accordingly lasts much longer.

I do not know whether Common prawns have any special preferences by way of bait. But you would, doubtless be able to capture them with fresh fish heads until you discover any particular tastes by inquiry and experiment.

Bait used by professional fishermen to capture whelks on grounds between Grimsby, South Humberside and Hythe, Kent includes salted cod heads, herring, skate, dogfish, shark and crushed mussels. Shore crabs are also used, sometimes mixed in the bait strings with salt fish. These crabs can not only be caught in a hoop net but, when crushed and put into a small bag of shrimp netting, be used as bait in a hoop net. So they are the most easily procured bait of all.

Grounds

Lobsters are to be found on rocky or stony bottom at any depth all round the coast of the British Isles. And, in theory, if you were to pinpoint a patch of rough ground by examination of an Admiralty or fishing chart and/or using your echo sounder, you could set a trap or two there and expect to catch them.

In practice, however, you would probably find traps already set there. They would belong to local lobster fishermen and it would be a waste of time to add to their number. If you did, it would not be long before the floats marking the position of your traps mysteriously disappeared. If they remained, you would seldom find lobsters in the traps when you lifted them.

If you are only going to lay, say, a couple of traps to catch shellfish for your own consumption, there is no need to encroach on grounds worked by professional fishermen. There are plenty of patches of rough close in to rocky coastlines and further offshore which it does not pay them to work. And these are the ones near which to lay your traps.

Lobsters are not inclined to move about as much as crabs and, I believe, if one locates an amenable hide-out with adequate food supplies and members of the opposite sex in its vicinity, it will remain there permanently. Discovery of such retreats is therefore a primary objective.

Wrecks are often used as lairs and, if they are shown on your chart and you can locate them, traps set close to them are likely to yield satisfactory catches.

Crabs range further than lobsters and travel considerable distances to slake their various appetites. They can be taken, like lobsters, on rock bottom and on sand, clay and mud as well. So precise positioning of traps is not so important if crabs are your principal quarry. Usual practice is to lay them anywhere in the vicinity of lobster grounds.

Dublin Bay prawns live on bottom composed of soft mud into which they can burrow, in depths between thirty and two hundred metres. Principal grounds around the British Isles are in the Irish Sea, off the coast of Northumberland, in the Firth of Clyde, Firth of Forth, Moray Firth and The Minches.

Whelks are to be found on grounds in estuaries and the open sea all round the coast of Britain and in commercial quantities on the East and South coasts. They may be found on any type of bottom but generally inhabit that composed of a mixture of mud, sand and shells. Those taken at sea are usually large and white-fleshed; those taken in estuaries may be small and dark-fleshed.

To lay traps

Assuming that you have rigged a couple of lobster traps with adequate lengths of line for the depth of water in which they are to be set, with an adequate number of floats and with adequate ballast in each to ensure that it will stay put in the strongest tide likely to be experienced, you can proceed to lay them.

As you approach the ground where you are going to lay them, there are two things to do: identify the landmarks by which you are going to be able to pinpoint it and either switch on your echo sounder or get the leadline ready for heaving.

When transits, confirmed by soundings, indicate that you are on the ground, make for one edge of it and, if it is rocky, lay your traps as near as possible to the rocks but just clear of them. If there is not much wind or tide, you may find it possible to lower a trap to the bottom and tow it gently to the edge of the rocks before letting go the float line. In clear, shallow water you may even be able to see the rocks and position the trap by eye instead of by touch.

Notes

Inkwell or other pots with the entrance through the top are likely to prove more effective than creels with eyes through the sides on grounds where there is much seaweed. There is less chance of their entrances becoming blocked.

Low, wide creels with low entrances are probably best for use on sand bottom where tides run strongly. Although observations by divers indicate that neither lobsters nor crabs are likely to enter any type of trap while the tide is running strongly, they are more likely to get washed off the sides of a top entrance pot when they do start to move about as the tide eases.

Lobsters and crabs have claws which are liable to drop through the bottom of a creel entrance if it is made of large mesh netting. When this happens they become tangled in the entrance and are often lost as the creel is hauled. It has been demonstrated that, if small mesh netting is fitted, catches improve.

The ideal place in which to fix bait is where a lobster or crab will try to get at it from a position close to the entrance; fixed to the inner side of the mouth of an inkwell pot, for instance. The most effective position to fix it would be near one side of a trap covered with netting for lobsters would try to get at it through the netting instead of the entrance. It is essential, when using traps covered with netting, that a lobster trying to reach the bait from the nearest point finds an entrance close to it.

About seventy per cent of the crabs landed in England and Wales are caught off the coasts of Northumberland, Yorkshire and Norfolk; about twenty per cent off Devon and Cornwall. They are caught all the year round in some places but mostly from April to July. Principal grounds are in depths of less than forty metres.

Crawfish are captured in commercial quantities mostly around the Scilly Islands and off the Cornish coast west of a line joining Padstow and the Lizard Head. They are taken between May and November, greatest catches usually being made in September.

Pots made of all-welded plastic tubing will withstand an immense amount of rough treatment

If they are to be used for catching prawns as well as lobsters, hoop nets are best made with small mesh spun nylon netting

You can make hoop nets quite easily yourself; you do not have to have any knowledge of net making to do so.

First of all get your local blacksmith to make you a couple of 600mm diameter hoops out of 16mm diameter iron rod. A hoop made of it is heavy enough to take the net straight down quickly and not too heavy to haul at high speed. Ideally it should be galvanised but black iron won't rust much if you give it a couple of coats of black varnish as soon as the hoops are made and, thereafter, give it additional coats from time to time.

If you are going to use your nets for catching lobsters, you can use 70mm mesh netting. But if you may want to use them for taking prawns and bait as well, it would be best to make them from small mesh prawn or shrimp netting.

Synthetic netting that will sink i.e. netting made from nylon twine is better than netting made from polythene or polypropylene twine. It won't tend to float up and about when a hoop is on the bottom and, possibly, scare fish away.

You will need enough netting to make a conical bag about 762mm deep, which will fit the hoops you have had made. And you will need some twine to lash the head of the netting to each hoop. Personally, I think spun nylon twine is best for the job. It has a rough surface and knots made with it will not slip. It is very strong and will not rot.

Whatever sort of twine you use, it is a simple job to lash netting to a hoop and lace the seams so that you have a conical bag. And when you have done that, the fastening of bait strings across the mouth of the net presents no problems. You simply tie two lengths of spun nylon or other stout twine, parallel to each other about 25mm apart, across the middle of the hoop.

Then usual practice is to punch two holes in circular pieces of leather about the size of a 50p piece and thread them on the strings so that they can be slid towards each other to hold bait. With seven such stoppers on the strings you can fix half-a-dozen pieces of bait between them securely.

Having added bait strings and stoppers to a net, the next thing to do is to fit a bridle and warp.

It is best to fit a three-legged bridle made of synthetic line which will float; it will then remain clear of the bait when the net is on the bottom. It is customary to make two of the legs with line of a lesser breaking strength than that of the third leg so that, if the hoop should get snagged, they will part and so increase chances of recovering it.

Having fitted bridles to hoops, all that remains to be done to make the nets ready for fishing is to attach warps to bridles. The warps are best made of floating rope and should be sufficient length for use in the depths of water in which you are likely to be working the nets.

If you are going to work them from your boat when at anchor, you will not need to attach floats to warps. But if you are going to lay them close in to a rocky shoreline, a couple of floats attached about two metres apart at the ends of the warps will enable you to recover the nets when you want.

You can use any of the types of bait that you would put in a lobster or prawn pot, in hoop nets, as long as you fasten it securely. Most people seem to leave them down for about twenty minutes before hauling. Then they give a gentle pull to take up any slack in the warp followed by a rapid pull until the catch is brought inboard.

Common prawns are to be found in the greatest quantities on sand and mud patches between rock outcrops where there is plenty of oarweed or eel grass. Traps should be laid as near large oarweeds as possible without being covered by them. They will catch prawns in daylight but will do so in greatest quantities at night.

Effective baits include fish heads, salt herring and gurnard, limpets and mussels but crushed green shore crabs are generally acknowledged to be the most attractive bait of all.

Prawns, like shrimps, are best boiled as soon as possible after they have been caught. It is recommended that they are put in briskly boiling water in batches small enough to allow them to move freely about in the water. After about seven minutes, they should be taken out and cooled in sea water or on sheets of canvas.

Should you ever want to lay lobster traps on a ground in an exposed position from which you may not be able to retrieve them for a few days because of the weather, you would find parlour pots most suitable for your purpose.

These have two compartments, one a reception chamber and the other a holding chamber.

Lobsters enter the former, in which the bait is fixed, through one or two side entrances. When they have satisfied their hunger and seek an exit, escape is apparently made easy for them by way of an entrance to the holding chamber. Once in the latter, escape is practically impossible.

A fisherman in the Isle of Wight once told me that most of the hen lobsters he was catching were full of a thick black substance in the head. He said that it smelt like oil, that it floated on water and that it remained after the lobsters were boiled. Crabs and prawns caught at the same time in the same area as the lobsters were not similarly affected.

He wanted to know what the substance was and I asked scientists at the MAAF Fisheries Laboratory in Burnham-on-Crouch and other lobster fishermen for their opinions on the matter.

Consensus was that, when large female lobsters with well-developed internal roes are cooked, it takes a considerable time for the heat to penetrate the thicker parts of the body sufficiently to change the black ovaries to a normal red colour. And, until complete cooking occurs, the ovary material remains soft and black.

The correctness of this theory can be tested very simply. All you have to do is to remove some of the black substance from a lobster's head and drop it in boiling water. If it quickly hardens and becomes red, the theory is correct.

If you catch any large hen lobsters which are somewhat soft, therefore, make sure that you boil them thoroughly before splitting them.

Dublin Bay prawns (Nephrops) are said to be averse to light and more likely to be found outside their burrows at dawn and dusk than in the daytime.

Shell casting and mating probably takes place around May for at this time catches are usually very low. In general, around the coasts of Britain, mature female nephrops spawn between August and October. At this time they carry black berries. They then disappear from catchable stocks until after their eggs are hatched in April or May. Soon afterwards they reappear among catches as 'softs'.

Around the coast of Scotland, highest catches are usually made in June, July, August and September. During these months they are captured in trawls as well as creels.

Nephrops creels are more lightly constructed than lobster creels, weighing only 5 kg, and most consist of galvanised steel frames covered by small mesh netting. The customary two entrances are made of similar netting and have metal or plastic eyes no more than 102 mm in diameter.

Creels with wooden bases are seldom used as they tend to sink in the mud at any angle. Bases are usually made of the same netting as is used to cover the rest of the creel as they are not likely to be damaged like the bases of lobster pots laid on rough ground. One end of a nephrops creel is usually hinged to form a large door from which the catch can be released speedily.

Although nephrops can be caught in lesser depths, creels are usually laid in depths of sixty metres or over to avoid entry of crabs which devour bait. They are baited with salt herring or mackerel, pieces of conger eel or dogfish. They may be hauled at intervals of a few hours or daily.

5. BEAM TRAWLING

A beam trawl is a conical net the headrope of which is attached to a beam or spar fitted to two iron heads or shoes which keep it above the seabed.

This type of trawl was devised for use in sailing vessels dependent solely on wind, tidal streams and currents for their motive power. In light airs, when they could make little way through the water, its mouth would remain open and it would continue to take fish.

When steam and internal combustion engines began to be installed in fishing boats, the beam trawl was superseded by the otter trawl which has a greater catching capacity as long as it is kept moving through the water continuously. But the beam trawl is still used for taking shrimps, soles, plaice and other flat fish by professional fishermen.

It consists of a beam, a pair of heads and a net comprising square, wings, belly and batings, pockets and a cod-end. A bridle is attached to the heads and a single warp is attached to the bridle for towing purposes.

In the heyday of the beam trawl, spars about fifteen metres long with a circumference of up to nearly a metre, were often used. Nowadays six metre beams are the longest used by professional shrimp fishermen; those wanting flat fish and shrimps for their own consumption only sometimes use trawls with beams no more than two metres in length.

Heads of up to 1.5 m high used to be used on large beam trawls. Nowadays they vary from 0.5–1 m, according to the length of the beam in use.

Gear

To work a beam trawl your basic requirements are a net complete with leaded groundrope, beam, a pair of iron heads or shoes of suitable size and a length of rope for making a bridle and a towing warp.

You are also likely to require a snatch block, several shackles, about four metres of braided nylon for a cod-line, a warp for a cod-end buoy line and a float or buff to attach to the latter. And, if you are going shrimping, you will need a riddle to sort your catches.

A trawl with a three metre beam will be about the largest you will be able to handle by yourself. Though you may never take a weight of fish in a larger trawl that you can't manage, you may not infrequently collect weights of weed and/or rubbish too great to be handled without risk of rupturing yourself.

Beam trawls designed for taking shrimp are almost exclusively made of small mesh nylon or polythene nowadays; those for taking soles, plaice, skate etc. of polythene or multifilament polypropylene.

If you are going to trawl mainly for flat fish and only occasionally for shrimps, your best choice would probably be a synthetic net with a spare small mesh nylon cod-end to attach instead of the standard cod-end when you go shrimping.

Trawl beams are usually made of a single spar of wood, either square or

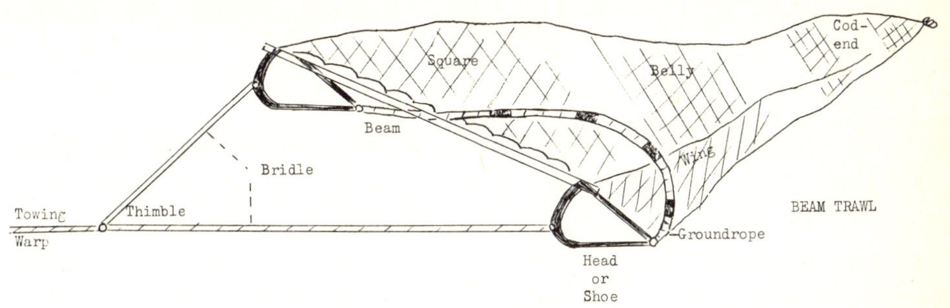

Components of a beam trawl

round, or a length of iron piping. But a leading supplier of fishing gear, as well as being able to supply such beams, can supply a special type of beam made of ash for use with its standard beam trawls. It is made in two halves, scarphed and bolted together with a fish plate in the middle.

This type of beam has advantages for use in small craft. It can be taken to pieces and the heads removed from it in a few minutes. The two halves, together with heads, net and warp, then require remarkably little stowage space.

You probably won't be able to get iron heads made by your local blacksmith more cheaply than you can buy them from the supplier of your trawl. So you may as well buy a pair of the size recommended by the latter, together with your trawl.

If you do not buy a bridle with your trawl, you will need a length of rope about twice the length of the beam for making one. And, unless you have a suitable length of rope for the purpose, it will probably be most convenient to use the same size and type of rope as for your towing warp and cod-end buoyline.

If, say, you are likely to be working mostly in depths from eight to twelve metres, you will need forty to sixty metres for your towing warp and twenty metres for your buoy line. Add another four metres for making a bridle and you are getting near enough to half a coil to make it an economic proposition to buy in this quantity. If you are going to haul by hand, you will want rope that you can grip firmly.

Use of an ample-sized snatch block, shackled to the mast or some position forward, will make hauling easier and will enable you to tow from forward –

the best procedure if there is risk of the trawl getting fast from time to time.

Use of a large, brightly-coloured float or buff will enable you to recover the cod-end buoy more easily in poor visibility if you get fast and have to cast off the towing warp. Such a float, too, will be more easily seen by other craft that might tow across you.

Rigging

If your boat is so arranged that you can carry your trawl on either port or starboard side decks, the direction of rotation of your propeller will indicate which to choose.

When you are hauling your trawl, you will find that your boat – particularly if it has a mast or much windage forward – will often lie quarter instead of beam on to wind and sea. When this happens the net, instead of coming in abeam, will tend to come in towards the quarter where it might foul your rudder and/or propeller.

If you have a right-hand turning propeller, and are working the net over

For heavy duty in deep water plastic floats usually have lugs on them

For general purpose use spherical plastic floats with two holes through the sides have much to commend them

the starboard side, a touch astern will counteract this tendency and, at the same time, swing the stern away from the net. For the same reason, it is best to work a trawl from the port side in a boat with a left-hand turning propeller.

Having assembled the beam and heads of your trawl ashore, and lashed the headrope to the beam and the wings to the after ends of the heads, you can put it on board. Having done so, you can lash a thimble in the middle of your bridle and then shackle each end of it to the forward end of a head.

Some operators of beam trawls shackle a block to the thimble in the middle of the bridle and reeve the towing warp through the block. This reduces labour when hauling by hand unless...unless a dirty great dollop of weed wraps itself around the block and effectively prevents the warp running through it at all!

If you are not working in weed-free waters, therefore, it is best to shackle one end of the towing warp to the thimble in the middle of the bridle and, unless the trawl is a small one which you can haul easily without the aid of any form of purchase, reeve it through a snatch block forward.

With the trawl stowed aboard, towing warp shackle on to the bridle, cod-end secured by a cod-line and buoy line attached to it, you are ready to go.

If the groundrope has enough lead on it in the first place, addition of chain is superfluous. If it hasn't, a length of chain wound around it improves a trawl's catching capability in my experience.

Grounds

Your choice of grounds will be dictated by tide and weather conditions and what intelligence you have been able to glean concerning the presence of your particular quarry in the locality.

Both pink and brown shrimps are to be found on various types of bottom from April to November in the Thames Estuary, Liverpool Bay and the Ribble, Morecambe Bay, the Solway Firth, the Wash and other areas of shoal water around the coast.

Pink shrimps are to be found on hard ground and, at certain times of the year, on mud patches on hard ground and/or if you travel along a hard bottom and mud boundary, known as an edge. They do not frequent clean, sandy bottom.

Brown shrimps are to be found on sand or mud bottom and, sometimes, along an edge.

The most favourable tidal conditions in which to trawl for shrimps are those which prevail for two or three days after the lowest neap tides start to 'make' into spring tides. The colour of the water is all-important. Neither pink nor brown shrimps are likely to be taken in quantity in clear water so, during neap tides, a breeze is necessary to stir things up. During springs it may not be possible to trawl for them except at high and low water.

Soles, plaice, flounders, skates, rays and other flat fish are to be found on sand, shingle and mud bottom from March to October off almost every part of the UK coast. You cannnot find them with an echo sounder but, by observing the grounds frequented by established fishermen and the catches they land, you will get a good idea of the best grounds to try for a start.

Thereafter, if you keep your eyes and ears wide open, you won't have much doubt about which grounds will be the best to work in different conditions of wind and weather.

Shooting and Hauling

Having reached your chosen ground with your trawl rigged and ready for shooting, the next thing to do is to get it on the bottom without delay.

I have seen it advocated in writing that, when shooting a beam trawl, you should let your boat lie broadside on to the direction in which you intend to tow. Personally, I prefer to keep a little way on so that the cod-end buoy and line, net and beam are carried well clear and the boat remains manoeuvrable all the time. It is not difficult, with the aid of the bridle, to ensure that the beam remains the right way up and that all is in order for the net to sink, before you start paying the warp out.

If you shoot a net made of buoyant materials, such as polyethylene or polypropylene, from a practically stationary boat, there is always a risk of its cod-end floating up and getting foul of the beam and/or heads. But, if you proceed slowly across the tide while you are shooting, and turn gradually so that you are heading down tide before you start paying away, you run little risk of this happening.

Having shot away your trawl without any risk of its capsizing before reaching the bottom and paid out a length of warp three to five times the depth of water you are working in, it is advisable, as you gradually increase speed down tide, to make sure that the heads are, in fact, being towed along the bottom. You can do this by laying a hand on the warp, the feel of which will soon tell you whether they are on or off the seabed.

Beam trawls were designed for use by sailing vessels liable to become becalmed or to make little way in light airs. They will take soles and shrimps at slow speeds and there is no need to waste fuel by towing over grounds at more than two knots, except perhaps towards the end of a tow when an increase of speed may serve to carry them down into the cod-end.

In calm weather, when your trawl is on the bottom and you have adjusted engine revolutions so as to maintain a suitable speed, there is little to do except keep the boat on a course that will take the trawl over the ground that you want it to cover and keep an eye on the cod-end float.

If the latter disappears from sight, as it is likely to do when you have got a new net and are towing it against the tide to tighten the knots, you may be towing through the water at too great a speed for the trawl to remain on the bottom. That doesn't matter much when the principal object of the operation is to tighten the knots but it matters a lot when you are after fish.

Then, the only thing to do if the float disappears, is to reduce engine revolutions until you can see it again and to assure yourself that the heads are on the bottom by the feel of the warp.

How long should a beam trawl be towed before it is hauled? The answer to that one is that it is impossible to lay down any hard and fast rules for the duration of a tow. The best results are likely to be obtained by trying out a ground with a tow of short duration first and then adjusting the length of subsequent tows as circumstances dictate.

Whatever length of time you decide to tow, the moment will arrive when

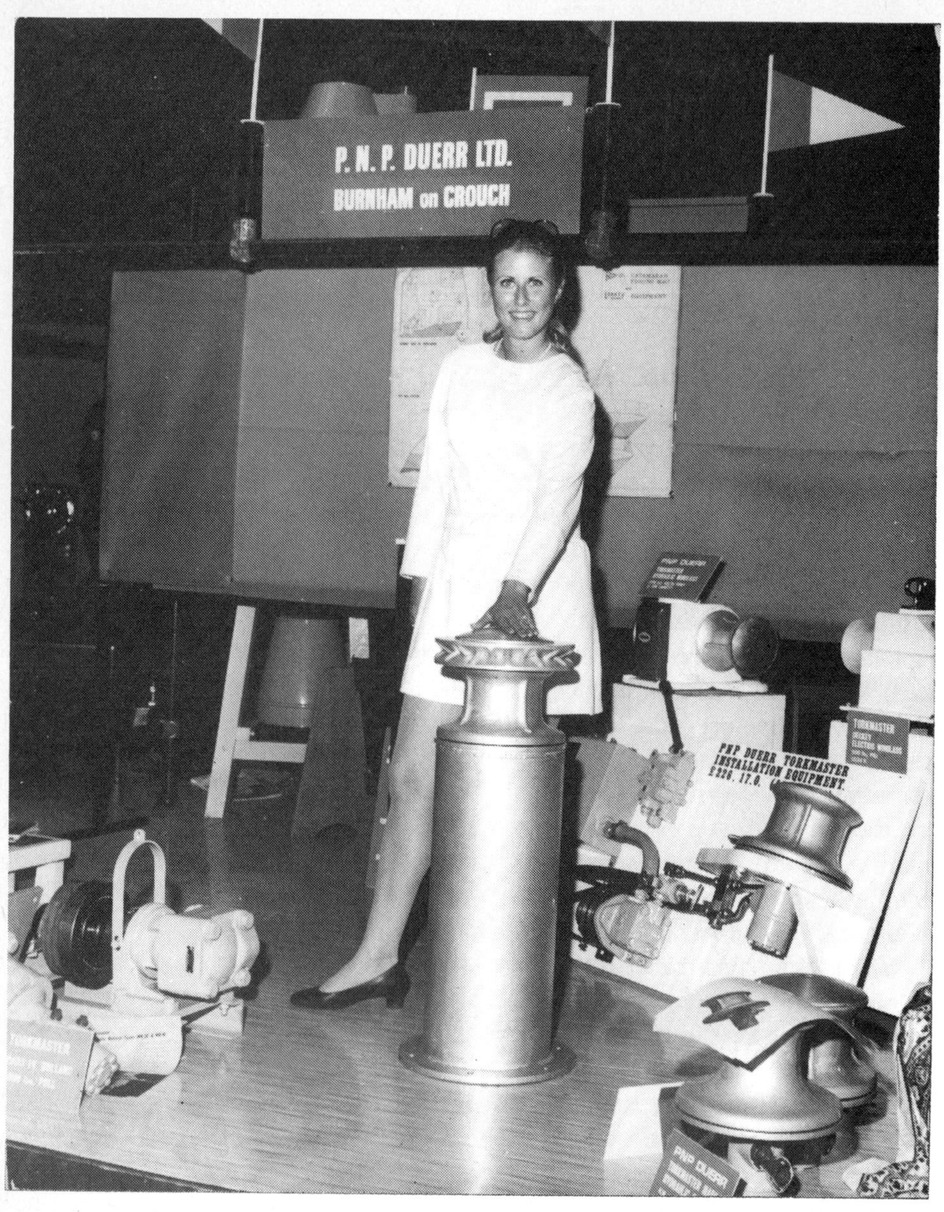

A line hauler is a desirable item of equipment in a boat used for beam trawling

you decide to haul. And this is the time to increase revolutions and tow at increased speed for a minute or two. Underwater photographs of towed trawls invariably show that some fish swim along just ahead of the groundrope for several minutes before either accelerating and getting away from it altogether or reducing speed and allowing themselves to be caught. If you increase your speed just before hauling, you stand a chance of catching some of these as well as of shifting those already in the body of the trawl towards the cod-end.

Hauling a small beam trawl is not a difficult operation except in certain conditions of tide and wind. Say you have been towing down tide and wind at two and a half to three knots over the ground and have increased speed to four knots for a minute before you are ready to start, the first thing to do is to put your gear in neutral and alter course to bring the trawl abeam on whichever side of the boat you normally stow it.

The boat will then lie broadside on to the sea and be carried away from the net by wind and tide so that the warp lies approximately at right angles to the fore and aft line. When all way is off the boat and these conditions prevail, you can start hauling and continue to haul away until the bridle appears. Then, if two men are available, each can take a leg of the bridle and haul on it until the heads and beam are on the surface. A lift by each will bring the heads inboard and, after that, the groundrope can be lifted over the rail so that there is no further possibility of fish escaping from the net.

If you are by yourself, getting the heads and beam inboard is not quite so simple a matter. You have to get one of the heads inboard and jamb or lash it so that it won't shift and then get the other which has, of course, disappeared below the surface again. Only when you have got them both can you attend to the groundrope and be sure of capturing all the fish in the net

More often than not, ideal conditions of wind and tide do not prevail when you come to haul a beam trawl. The wind may freshen against the tide so that the movement of the boat when beam on is chiefly affected by the former, while the trawl is affected only by the latter, and you have to haul at speed to prevent the trawl being carried under the keel. The wind may prevent you lying beam on to the tide for more than a few seconds, making it necessary to maintain your position with the engine. In fact, there are a whole host of differing circumstances that may call for expert seamanship and ship handling when hauling.

The same skills may be called for when you find yourself hauling involuntarily – when the trawl gets foul of some obstruction on the seabed. In such an event, the boat's progress is usually halted and the screw begins to churn the water up to draw your attention to the fact. Then, the only thing to do is to buoy the end of your towing warp and let it go before turning, picking up the cod-end float line and towing it in the reverse direction to the previous path of the trawl.

Having hauled your trawl and got the cod-end inboard, it is best to release the catch into a lined well, pounds or containers from which crabs and small fish cannot escape into the bilges. Once there, they are just about impossible to extract and the bilge will become malodorous or, in other words, stink to high heaven.

CHAPTER TWO

Fish

HABITS AND HABITATS

Bass

Bass enter estuaries and rivers from Lincolnshire around the South Coast of England to Wales in spring and remain until late autumn. They grow to a size of about 8 kg. Among their favourite foods are small crustaceans and sand-eels for which they search in broken water around sand and shingle banks.

Cod and Cod-like Species

When caught in British waters the Cod is a greenish or brown-greenish colour with brown or yellow spots. It grows to a length of 1.2 m and a weight of 45 kg. For marketing purposes it is customarily divided into four size ranges. When it is over 760 mm long, it is called a Cod; between 635 and 737 mm a Sprag; between 533 and 610 mm a Codling; and between 305 and 508 mm a Small Codling.

Next to the cod the most important member of the cod family is the Haddock which also has a barbel on its lower lip but has a deeper, brown coloured back and black blotches above its pectoral fins. It grows to a length of over 900 mm and a weight of over 11 kg but few haddock of over 610 mm long are normally captured.

The Coalfish or Saithe resembles the cod in having three dorsal and two anal fins and, during the first year or two of its life, in having a barbel too. But as it grows older, its lower jaw becomes larger than its upper one and the barbel atrophies. The coalfish is slenderer than the cod, has a blue-black back and a white lateral line. It grows to a length of over a metre and a weight of about 15 kg.

After it is about a year old the coalfish prefers to frequent deep water and is mostly found off the northern coasts of Scotland. In this respect it differs from the Pollack or Lythe which is seldom taken in depths greater than eighty metres. The latter is distinguishable from the coalfish by its blue-

Bass weighing up to about 5 lb (2.3 kg) can be taken in 4 in. (102 mm) mesh gill nets

brown colouring, lack of barbel and even more prominent lower jaw. It grows to a length of about 610 mm and a weight of 4 kg.

Cod, haddock, coalfish and pollack are all clearly recognisable members of the cod family (Gadidae). Another important member of it is not. The Ling is a long, narrow fish with a barbel but only one anal and two dorsal fins. It is olive-brown dashed with blue and grows to a length of over two metres.

Similar in some respects to the ling is the Tusk which is found in deep water to the north of Scotland. It has a barbel, one long dorsal and one long anal fin, and brown-yellow bands on back and sides. It grows to a length of one metre.

The Whiting, although its barbel atrophies as it grows, is also a member of the cod family. It is the most delicate tasting member and is caught in most coastal waters. It grows to a weight of about 2 kg.

Author with cod caught in a trammel net within a cable's length of his moorings in the River Deben

Cod

Haddock

Coalfish

Pollack

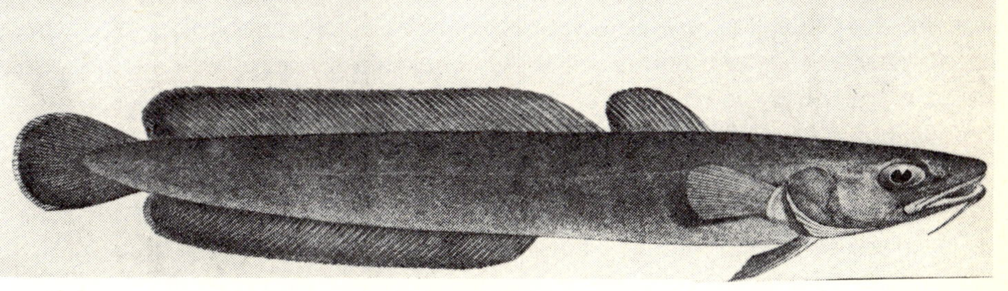

Ling

Whiting

Cuttlefish and Co.

The Common Cuttlefish (*Sepia officinalis*) belongs to a class of molluscs known as Cephalopoda which also includes octopus and squid.

Unlike the octopus, it progresses entirely by swimming. It has a large bulky head bearing two large eyes and ten sucker-covered arms, its fleshy body being supported by a skeleton of chalk-like consistency – the so-called bone. Its back is normally dark brown, striped with white, but is continually changing shade either to match its surroundings or as an expression of its emotions.

If a small fish or crustacean swims within reach, two specially-long arms are suddenly shot out, the suckers securing themselves to the prey. The arms retract to bring the food to the mouth where a parrot-like beak crushes it to pieces. Hunting food may be carried out while stationary in the water or swimming slowly, avoiding action by ejecting a jet of water from the mantle and darting backwards at high speed. While performing the latter manoeuvre, a cloud of dense black ink may be thrown out as a screen against a predator.

Cuttlefish lay large gelatinous eggs, enclosed in an elastic membrane, which are fixed in grape-like clusters to leaves of *Zostera marina* or other suitable surfaces. The young cuttlefish develops inside the capsule until fully formed and then breaks its way out. Cuttlefish are likely to be caught wherever around the coast there remain beds of zostera or similar weed.

The body of the Common Octopus (*Octopus vulgaris*) is bag-like with a pair of large eyes and eight long arms furnished with two rows of suckers. Its food consists to a great extent of crabs which are seized by the arms and crushed with the aid of a hard beak. Its body is usually pale but, when disturbed, rapidly darkens in colour.

The octopus lurks in crevices, occasionally crawling over rocks in search of food. At times it swims for short distances, propelling itself by a jet of water expelled from the mantle cavity. Its eggs are laid in grape-like clusters attached to rocks, the young emerging as small, fully-formed octopi. It grows to a size of about 600 mm across the body and tentacles. It is sometimes captured on the South Coast of England but not elsewhere in the British Isles.

Squid (*Toradodes sagittatus*), which grow to about 400 mm long are more streamlined than cuttlefish and do not have a bone in their bodies. Their two-eyed heads are narrower and, in addition to eight short arms projecting from their topknots, have two permanently extended arms. These they no doubt use to seize their prey as does a cuttlefish.

They can eject ink screens and jet propel themselves in a similar way, and may be able to manoeuvre more swiftly as they have what you might call lateral fins on either side towards the base of their bodies. Like their cousins, they are edible and also make excellent bait. They are to be found all round the British Isles.

Dogfish

Four species of dogfish are found in British waters: the Spur, also known as the Spiny or Spiked Dog; the Greater Spotted, also known as the Bull Huss; the Lesser Spotted, also known as the Huss; and the Smooth Hound Dogfish. They are all sharks and the larger species grow to a length of up to 1.5m.

One stock of spur dogs winters on grounds in the South Western Approaches and sections of it migrate up-Channel and north along the East Coast every summer. Other sections migrate northwards into the Irish Sea during the summer months. Another stock of spur dogs inhabits an area from the West Coast of Scotland to the Norwegian coast.

Spur dogs which, incidentally, are so called because they have a sharp spur or spike in front of each dorsal fin, do not spend practically all their time close to the bottom like the other species of dogfish but are to be found at all depths. Greater Spotted dogs are most frequently found over rocky bottom and are often caught on lines set for conger eels. Lesser Spotted dogs are said to favour sandy bottom while Smooth Hounds may be found over sand, shell and even mud bottom.

Dogfish

Dogfish are said to prefer oily baits such as pieces of pilchard, mackerel or herring but you can catch them on handlines at a very fast rate with practically any type of bait when large numbers are around your boat. They are such voracious feeders that they will sometimes swallow one bait and then swim along the line and take another as well.

Garfish

Garfish (*Belone belone*) are found in all waters around the British Isles but more often off southern than northern coasts. They have slender, silver bodies up to about 760 mm long and beaks like those of swordfishes in miniature. For this reason they are also known as swordfishes (in Scotland) and long-noses. Green-bones is another name for them because their backbones are a distinct green colour.

Some people will not eat them because they think that the green tinge you see after you have gutted and cleaned them permeates the flesh and that the latter must therefore be a bit off. But this cannot be the case with freshly caught fish and the flesh of these is in fact delectable.

Garfish usually come inshore in summer a little earlier than mackerel and for this reason are sometimes known as Mackerel Guides. They are to be found singly and in shoals and when they are shoaling can be detected with a fish-finding echo sounder. They feed mostly on whitebait, small pilchards, herring etc.

Before echo sounders were installed in fishing boats, some fishermen used to locate them by scattering twigs or straw on the surface in places where they thought garfish might be. The latter apparently like to play around and even leap over such jetsam.

It is said that garfish are very fast swimmers and that it is their speed when pursuing their prey that usually causes them to leap right out of the water. Presumably it's the speed they use to escape pursuit that causes them to leap out on some occasions.

I have been told that there is usually a big run of them up the English Channel in May; that they congregate in fast water in the lee of headlands in whatever depth their feed is; that you will find shoals with no mackerel among them but seldom shoals of mackerel without a few garfish in company; that both species depart for warmer waters in September or October.

The species can be caught by bobbing with long staples of cotton or other vegetable fibres laid together and doubled back with both free ends whipped on to the end of a line. They are caught in commercial quantities in beach seines when shoals come close inshore. And they are caught in considerable numbers by sea anglers who have taken the trouble to study their reactions to proffered baits and lures closely.

Halibut

There are three principal species of halibut: the Atlantic Halibut (*Hippoglossus hippoglossus*), the Pacific Halibut (*Hippoglossus stenolepsis*) and the Greenland Halibut (*Reinhardtius hippoglossoides*) which is often called Mock Halibut.

The halibut is the largest flat fish of all and in European waters is found in the greatest numbers to the north of the British Isles. It is a deep water species frequently caught around Iceland and the Faroe Islands. Specimens up to 250 kg have been caught and some authorities consider that it grows to a weight of about 350 kg. All halibut weighing over 25 kg are females.

The body of a halibut is thicker and narrower than that of most flat fish. The back is usually a dark olive or brown colour and the belly white. It has a large sharp-toothed mouth and its principal prey are said to be haddock, whiting, soles, dabs, *Nephrops norvegicus* (Dublin Bay prawns) and squid.

Atlantic Halibut spawn in the spring to the west of the Faroe Islands. They migrate to inshore waters around the Shetland and Orkney Islands and the north of Scotland in June and July. They also visit grounds off the west and south coasts of Ireland but those caught on them are usually smaller than those taken in deep water north of Scotland.

Small halibut have been taken on sand or rock bottom in a few fathoms off the north coast of Scotland but large ones rarely in less than fifty metres. They are said to prefer a sea water temperature of between one and six degrees Centigrade and to frequent the edges of hard ground.

Herring

Until a few years after the 1939/45 war herring used to arrive in Shetland Isles waters in the spring and then travel down the east coasts of Scotland and England. Drifters from Great Yarmouth and Lowestoft, as well as huge fleets of smaller Scottish drifters, used to go north to intercept them and to prey on them throughout their long journey to the Dover Strait.

In the spring they used to use Lerwick as a base, then such ports as Fraserburgh, Peterhead and Aberdeen and then, when the herring came south of the border, North Shields, Scarborough and Whitby. Although some operated from Grimsby in August and September, the majority of East Anglian and Scottish drifters worked from Yarmouth once the main shoals were to be found south of the Humber.

The first full moon in October used to be D-Day for the East Anglian onslaught on the herring. Scottish girls by the trainload used to arrive in Yarmouth to split and barrel the enormous landings that used to be made until the herring reached the Sandettie Bank in early December and the season came to an end.

Thereafter the Scottish fleet used to return north and go through the Caledonian Canal to continue pursuing herring in the Minches. There, smaller craft had been drifting for them all summer while ring-netters had usually been making a satisfactory living capturing them in the Firth of Clyde.

After Christmas the East Anglian drifters used to go to the south coast of Ireland for the herring fishing from Dunmore East. And then some of them would drift for mackerel off Cornwall before going north to Shetland again in the spring.

Nowadays no big drifters are based in East Anglian or Scottish ports. Pelagic trawling and purse-seining for herring have proved to be more profitable methods of catching them than drifting as they can be captured by day when they are close to the bottom as well as by night when they rise to the surface. The centuries old North Sea drift net fishery, therefore, no longer exists.

Large Species

At least fifteen species of skates and rays, most of which grow into big fish, frequent British waters. Those you are most likely to come across are Common Skates, Long-nosed Skates, Thornback Rays (Roker) and Sting Rays.

Common Skates weighing over 182 kg have been caught occasionally and over 83 kg not infrequently. They are usually to be found in deeper water than Thornback Rays which grow up to about 26 kg. Long-nosed skates up to 1.5 m long usually frequent deep water but Sting Rays may be found in shallow water. If you do boat one of the latter, it would be prudent to proceed with caution until all danger of a collision between you and its tail is past.

Tuna, formerly known as Tunny in this country, may be encountered in plenty in the North Sea northwards of the latitude of Flamborough Head. And when warm water reaches the south-west coasts of England and Ireland, they may be encountered in those areas as well. Largest tuna caught on a line in the North Sea turned the scales at 386 kg but one stranded on the beach at Walton-on-Naze, Essex in 1928 weighed 427 kg.

It used to be thought that only an odd Swordfish or two strayed into British waters when unusually warm currents made it amenable for them to do so. But recent sightings indicate that they may visit the area in greater numbers. Whatever their visitations, however, you are likely to encounter Marlin only occasionally.

The Conger Eel is another large species frequently caught in British waters. One weighing 44 kg was caught by line off Brixham several years ago and a specimen weighing 46 kg was caught in a trawl off Eyemouth in 1963. Largest conger on record is a 2.7 m female weighing 73 kg caught in 1904.

Herring being shaken from a drift net

Herring

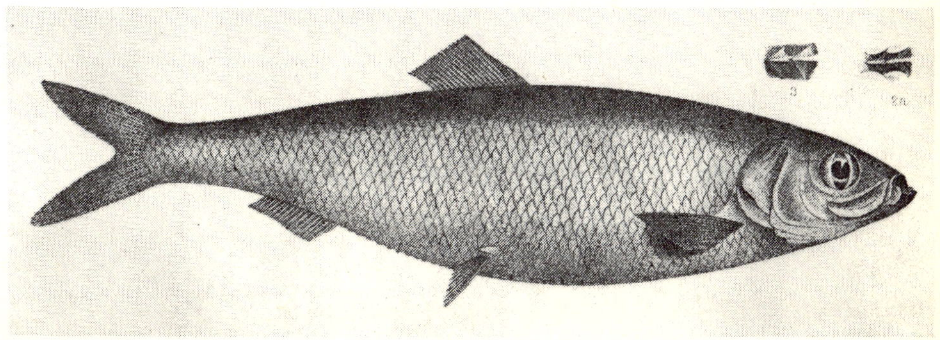

Tuna are one of the most valuable species of fish that can be taken on trolled lines

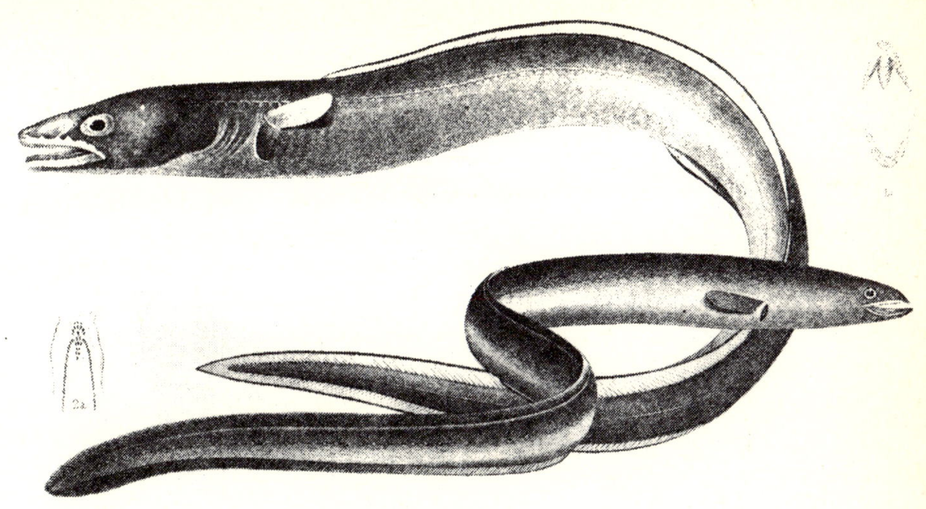

Conger eels

It is possible that you will capture at one time or another a big fish (up to 2.4 m long) which looks something like a skate but is actually a shark. If you cannot immediately identify it, it is likely to be a Monk or Angel fish.

Mackerel

Most mackerel taken on the south and south-west coasts of England and in the Irish Sea are of Celtic Sea stock.

These mackerel spawn in the shallow waters of the continental shelf in spring and migrate to inshore waters in search of food – whitebait and sand-eels as well as planktonic organisms such as Copepods.

In late autumn they start to concentrate in huge shoals to winter south of the Eddystone.

Mackerel of this stock over 460 mm long weighing more than about 2 kg are rarely taken but a specimen 620 mm long weighing over 23 kg was landed at Newlyn in Cornwall in 1973.

Porpoises, Dolphins and Whales

Porpoises are distinguished from dolphins, when they are in the water, by their heads and back fins. Porpoises have round heads and triangular back fins. Dolphins have heads with a well-defined beak and sickle shaped back fins. If you can examine one of them out of the water, it will be a porpoise if it has spade-shaped teeth, a dolphin if its teeth are pointed.

They are both related to Killer Whales because they are members of the Family Delphinidae, a family which embraces all toothed whales. It is a very large family including the Killer Whale or Grampus, the Narwhal, White and Pilot Whales. Although called whales these are in fact huge dolphins.

Killer whales are among the largest members of the family. They grow to a length of about 9.5 m and have blunt, rounded snouts. They have long dorsal fins, often visible above water, and big broad pectoral fins. Backs are black and bellies white, and they have white or pale yellow spots on their bodies. They have been known to hunt in schools of up to one hundred individuals.

They were originally so called because they attack baleen and maybe other whales. They can swim at speed up to 37 kph and have strong teeth which enable them to tear huge pieces of flesh and the tongues, which they particularly relish, from other whales.

There are scores of smaller members of Fam. Delphinidae, all called either porpoises or dolphins but with such imprecision as to cause confusion. What we in England, for instance, call the Bottle-Nosed Dolphin, Americans call the Common Porpoise. It is a large dolphin, which may grow to a length of 3.6 m, with a short beak. Its back is black, grey or brown and its belly white.

What we call the Common Porpoise is black on the back and white underneath. It has a round head without a beak, a triangular back fin and never grows to a length of more than two metres. Our Common Dolphin is black on the back, white underneath with – between the two – a lateral strip of mixed grey, white and yellow. It grows to a length of 2.4 m. It feeds on pilchards, herrings and sardines, its prediliction for the latter perhaps causing it to frequent warmer waters than the porpoise.

Salmon

Generally speaking Atlantic salmon ascend British rivers in spring, summer and early autumn, and are then known as clean salmon on account of their bright, well-fed appearance. Spawning takes place, with rare exceptions, between the beginning of September and the middle of January.

The hen fish lays her eggs on a bed of coarse gravel with a down-flow of cold, clean water, and buries them in it. The eggs hatch early in the year. The little fish, called Alevins are still attached to their yolk-sac and shun the light so long as it lasts.

When the days lengthen and there is more food in the water, the yolk-sacs are finished and the young fish seek the light, coming to the surace of the gravel and starting to feed. They are then called Fry.

During their first summer they grow and, at a not well defined point, are called Parr. Parr resemble small trout, except that a row of dark blotches, or parr-marks, down their sides, are generally more pronounced.

Parr remain in fresh water for anything from one and a half to three and a half years, depending on water temperatures and food supply. When ready to go to sea, they become bright silvery and are called Smolts. Most smolts are about 127 mm long and weigh about 60 gm.

All the year's production of smolts migrate downstream together to the sea in late spring, generally on a heavy flood. Where they go when they leave the rivers has long been a matter for conjecture. But catches off Greenland indicate that some migrate northwards and there is evidence to indicate that some do so to feed on shrimps under the Arctic ice.

The first fish to re-appear as adults return to the rivers as Grilse the following summer, after one winter at sea. Most weigh between two and four

*Sea Trout (*Salmo trutta*)*

Salmon (Salmo salar)

kilos but larger and smaller grilse are not uncommon.

Salmon are fish which have spent two or more winters in the sea. Whatever time of year a salmon enters a river, it will remain there without digesting any food until the back-end, before spawning.

After spawning, grilse and salmon are called Kelts. The great majority die, cock fish immediately after spawning and hen fish on their way downstream or in the sea. Very few fish spawn twice. The size of a fish depends on the number of winters it has spent in the sea before returning to spawn.

The Atlantic salmon grows to a length of about 1.4m. It is caught with rod and line, and with less legitimate devices, in rivers; with gill nets in the lower reaches of rivers; with draw, trammel and bag nets in estuaries; and with longlines as well as gill nets at sea.

The salmon is defined in the Salmon and Freshwater Fisheries (Protection) (Scotland) Act 1951 as including 'all migratory fish of the species Salmo salar and Salmo trutta and commonly known as salmon and sea trout respectively'.

Tope

The tope is a small shark. It is edible and is sold for human consumption in some countries. Specimens up to 38kg and three metres long have been caught in British waters but the majority taken vary in weight between 9kg and 23kg, and in length between one metre and two metres.

Some tope remain all the year round and are taken occasionally on long-lines. They are captured all round the British Isles but in diminishing numbers in higher latitudes and never above sixty degrees north. They are said to migrate southwards into warmer water or offshore into deeper water in winter.

It is probable that tope visit shallow water in the English Channel in the spring to breed as, between mid-May and mid-June, most of them caught there are females with young. During the latter half of June and in July, catches consist mostly of males but in August big female tope – some with young – are not infrequently captured.

They are caught on lines by baiting one or two hooks with whole mackerel, whiting or squid. They cannot be taken by trolling lures.

Venomous Species

Among venomous species you may catch are Spiny Dogfish which get around both singly and in shoals. This small shark, which grows to a length of about 1.2m, has a poison gland at the base of its dorsal fin which can inflict a very painful wound.

Sting rays may be caught when the water is warm. They grow to a length of 600mm with a tail about 380mm long and they can use the latter to inflict severe, sometimes poisonous, wounds.

You might encounter a venomous octopus, or one which could wound by biting you, at any time. And you might boat a conger eel which would be likely to wound by biting you but perhaps by biting and poisoning; the species has a poison gland associated with the teeth.

You might boat a Sea Urchin or two from time to time. If any of their spines penetrate your hands, you are likely to suffer no more than severe pain but some species are venomous and capable of inflicting serious wounds.

The only other species likely to menace you, should you wade in shallow water in rope soled shoes or bare feet, is the Lesser Weever fish. It grows to a length of about 150mm and has a habit of burying itself in the sand with only the top of its head and its dorsal fin showing. At the base of the latter is a poisonous gland.

Preferred Water Temperatures

The British Isles are situated where two fish distribution zones overlap. The northern zone extends from the sub-Arctic to the English Channel and species characteristic of it include cod and cod-like species, herring and salmon. Northern extremity of the southern zone is a line running from the Thames Estuary to the north-west coast of Ireland. South of this line characteristic species are, pilchard, bass and grey mullet.

Scientific investigations have shown that, although cod and haddock prefer to be in water between 2° and 4°C and are not infrequently found in water up to 10°C, you are most unlikely to catch them in water above that temperature. They have shown, too, that herring prefer water between 3½° and 7½°C.

Salmon are said to prefer temperatures between 4 and 10°C and halibut temperatures between 2° and 5°. Hake (11°–19°), mackerel (12°–18°) and tuna (14°–22°) prefer warmer waters.

Scientific investigations have revealed too that herring spawn in water between 0° and 12° in spring, and between 8° and 15° in autumn; plaice in water between 4° and 7° in the North Sea; pilchards in water between 9° and 16° in the English Channel; and mackerel in water between 10° and 15° in the North Atlantic.

Minimum temperature at which lobsters start to move about in search of food is known too. They become active only when the temperature has reached 10°C in spring.

Stocks

According to D. J. Garrod and M. J. Holden of the Fisheries Laboratory at Lowestoft, who have made special studies of the stocks on which inshore longline fisheries are based, inshore cod fisheries are all based on migratory stocks which appear at different points along the coast according to season.

On the South Coast catches are made from a single 'Channel' stock which appears in winter off Beachy Head and during summer all along the South Coast.

There is also a winter fishery for pre-spawning cod in the Straits of Dover, but catches made there are from a different group of cod which inhabits the southern part of the North Sea. The group spends the summer in deep water on the southern edge of the Dogger Bank and in winter migrates to spawning grounds in the southern part of the North Sea. One and two year old codling from this stock migrate to the coasts of Norfolk and Suffolk in autumn and winter, and are caught on longlines.

Cod caught off the North East Coast form one of the truly inshore stocks of fish likely to be caught by means of lines. Very few of them that have been tagged have been re-captured more than twenty-five miles offshore.

This group migrates mainly between the Tyne area, where it supports the summer North Shields and Hartlepool fisheries, and Flamborough Head, where catches are made in the winter line and trawl fisheries. In some winters it moves as far south as the River Humber.

Inshore whiting fisheries are similar to those for cod. Stocks of this species are distributed in the same way and have similar migratory habits. But they are more abundant on the West and South Coasts than elsewhere.

Whiting spawning and nursery grounds lie east of the Isle of Man, off Conway, in Liverpool Bay and from the Solway Firth to St Bees Head. There is also a ground west of the Isle of Man, off the coast of Co. Down.

Haddock fisheries are in some ways similar to those for cod in that inshore catches are made from migratory stocks. But this species does not form so many separate groups as do cod and whiting, and is mainly concentrated in the central and northern parts of the North Sea.

Spur dogfish winter on grounds in the South Western Approaches and migrate up Channel and north along the East Coast every summer. They can be caught on longlines all along the South and East Coasts while they are migrating. They also migrate northwards into the Irish Sea during the summer months.

Skates, rays and roker form 'resident' inshore groups. In the North Sea they inhabit grounds extending from the Wash southwards. As water temperatures rise in the spring, they move inshore to spawn and can be taken on longlines from April to July. When water temperatures begin to fall, they return to deeper water.

In the Irish Sea they spawn and inhabit nursery grounds off the English and Welsh coasts before moving slowly across to the Irish coast as they grow older.

CHAPTER THREE

Fishing

QUESTIONS AND ANSWERS

Know your Ropes

'I am currently fitting out a boat which I hope to use for beam trawling, potting and longlining. And it is clear that I am going to have to purchase considerable quantities of rope of various sizes. I am absolutely bewildered by the variety of cordage now offered by ship chandlers in this country and would much appreciate it if you could give me a brief review of ropes now available which are designed for use in small craft.'

As vegetable fibre ropes are still available and favoured for some purposes in small craft, let's have a look at them first.

Cheapest of all fibre ropes is Coir or Bass rope, which is often used for the groundrope of beam trawls. It is made from the fibres of coconut husks and is light, elastic and durable in salt water. Sisal, made from the fibres of the Agave grown in East Africa, continues to be used to some extent. It is almost as strong as manila and can be used for the same purposes. Manila hemp rope, made from the fibres of the plant *Cannabis sativa* which is grown in the Philippines, is the strongest and most durable of all vegetable fibre ropes and does not swell when wet.

Principal synthetic ropes designed and manufactured in the UK for use in small craft are made from nylon (polyamide 66) international symbol for which is PA, Terylene (polyester) – PES, polythene (polyethylene) – PE, and polypropylene – PP.

Before I endeavour to give you some idea of their different properties, I had better explain methods of rope construction. Cordage made from natural fibres is made by combing them, spinning them into yarns, twisting the yarns into strands, and twisting or plaiting the stands into the final product. Vegetable fibres grow in certain lengths (staples) from a few centimetres in the case of cotton to as much a half a metre in the case of hemp or flax.

Synthetic fibres can be extruded in filaments of any length and consequently types of cordage, previously impossible to make, are available today.

There are, for instance, twisted monofilament polythene and polypropylene ropes, twisted multifilament and staple spun polypropylene ropes, twisted multifilament and staple spun nylon and polyester ropes. (Staple spun ropes are made from filaments which have been chopped into short lengths (staples) and then twisted into yarns, strands and ropes.) There are also split film polypropylene ropes – ropes made from a film of the material, split under tension into filaments which are then twisted into strands and ropes.

Three strand nylon ropes are about twice as strong as manila ropes of equivalent size. Not only three strand but plaited nylon ropes and ropes made from spun nylon are popular for use in small craft. They are elastic, resistant to abrasion and attacks by bacteria etc. They sink in water. So do polyester ropes which are preferred to those made of nylon when non-stretch properties are required.

Polypropylene ropes are widely used in all forms of construction. They are considerably stronger than manila ropes and much more resistant to rot and abrasion. Unless a lead core is incorporated into them in the manufacturing process, they float. So do ropes made from polythene which are available in twisted monofilament form only.

A most satisfactory general purpose rope is one made from a combination of polypropylene and manila staples – the latter being proofed against rot. It is easy to handle, grip and splice, and possesses neutral buoyancy. It behaves like manila rope under normal conditions but is lighter, does not harden when wet and is more resistant to abrasion.

To Distinguish Synthetic Ropes

'Is there any way other than looking at it closely and feeling it, of distinguishing one type of synthetic rope from another?'

One way in which you may be able to discover whether a rope is made of polyamide (nylon), polyester (Terylene or Dacron), polyethylene, polypropylene or a mixture of, say, spun nylon and polypropylene or staple spun polypropylene and manila is to untwist a short length of it into yarns, burn individual yarns with a match and smell the smoke given off. Different types of fibre burn in different ways and produce smoke with different kinds of smell.

Before I describe these let me explain the abbreviations I am going to use – to avoid getting writer's cramp – for the various synthetic materials. They are symbols which have now been adopted internationally as they indicate the basic chemical substances from which the various fibres are composed. The symbol for nylon is PA; for Terylene or Dacron – PES; for polyethylene – PE; and for polypropylene – PP.

If you put a flame to vegetable fibres, they will burn rapidly and will continue to burn when the flame is removed. The smell of the smoke is similar to that of burning paper and the residue consists of fine ash.

When PA fibres are put into a flame they melt, burn with a light flame and give off white smoke. Yellowish drops drip from them and form into small, hard, round beads which are uncrushable. The smell of the smoke resembles that of celery. If the melting drops fall from the fibres, the latter cease to burn.

PES fibres melt and burn with a light flame which produces blackish smoke. Drops drip down and form small black beads which are uncrushable. Smoke given off has a slightly sweet, sooty smell. If the melting drops fall from the fibres, the latter cease to burn.

PE fibres shrink, curl, melt, burn with a light flame and form a hot melting substance – not beads – which cannot be stretched into a thread as hot melting PA and PES beads can. The residue is crushable. The smell resembles that of burning paraffin. If the melting substance drops from the fibres, the latter will continue to burn rapidly.

PP fibres shrink, melt, burn with a light flame and form a hot melting substance which can be stretched into fine thread. The residue consists of hard brown-black blobs which are not crushable. Smell resembles that of burning asphalt. When the melting substance drops from PP fibres, the latter will continue to burn slowly.

These characteristic reactions to flame make it possible – it's not so easy as it sounds – to discover the kind of fibres from which yarns or strands are made if they consist wholly of one kind. If fibres are mixed before being twisted into yarns, identification may be difficult.

Know your Nets

'When I retire next year I hope to buy a boat about ten metres long and do some fishing. I would be grateful for any information you can send me about the principal types of net used nowadays and what species they are used to catch.'

Nets mostly used nowadays include:

DRAFT NETS: nylon gill nets about 165 m long with a bag in the middle, used for catching salmon. Body of each net is made of 100 mm mesh and the wings of 127 mm mesh. Usually worked from sandbanks in an estuary in a somewhat similar way to beach seines.

DRIFT NETS: nets made with a mesh ranging between twenty-five rows per metre for gilling herring to sixty-five rows per metre for gilling sprats. They are usually made of nylon and are designed to hang vertically in the water.

FYKE NETS: conical, small mesh nets for capturing eels. They are about 3.5 m long and are held open by six or seven cane or plastic hoops varying in size from 600 mm to 200 mm diameter. From the centre of the 600 mm diameter entrance hoop extends a 600 mm x 4.5 m leader for diverting eels into the net and in the latter are three funnels for preventing their escape.

GILL NETS: nets with a mesh size ranging from 76 mm for catching small mullet and bass to 230 mm for catching cod. They are usually made of monofilament or twisted multifilament nylon and are so mounted on float and lead lines that they hang vertically in the water. Usual practice is to moor them in position but they are sometimes set free to drift.

HOOP NETS: conical nets about 760 mm long attached to cask hoops about 600 mm in diameter, used for catching lobsters, flat fish and common prawns. Bait strings are fitted aross the hoops to each of which is attached a bridle and warp for lifting from the seabed.

LANT NETS: seine nets made of very small (9 mm) mesh nylon netting, designed for catching sand eels.

SEINE NETS: nets used with long ropes attached to each wing end to draw bottom feeding fish to beach or boat. A BEACH SEINE or DRAW NET is shot in a semi-circle by a small boat rowing out from and returning to a beach, the ropes then being brought together and hauled. A DANISH SEINE is shot from a boat which motors round three legs of a triangle shooting warp-net-warp and then hauls either while moving ahead or at anchor. A PURSE SEINE is a net about 915 m long by 140 m deep used to encircle pelagic fish, the bottom of the net being pursed after encirclement to prevent the fish from escaping downwards.

SHANK NETS: nets designed to be towed by a boat or tractor, or drawn behind a horse and cart, in shallow water to catch shrimps. A typical net consists of a conical bag of shrimp netting about three metres long with its mouth attached to a wooden frame. The latter comprises a heavy beam about three metres long with a semi-circular arch above it made of bent willow.

STOW NETS: tapering box nets up to fifty-five metres long usually made in four sections. The leading section is made of large mesh netting, succeeding sections with meshes of diminishing size and the cod-end of very small mesh netting. The rectangular mouth of a stow net is opened and closed by two wooden baulks or spars about 5.5 m long. They are attached to headline and footline and the net is so constructed that they will be about six metres apart when it is fishing. This type of net is usually worked by boats anchored in a fairway to catch whitebait.

TANGLE NETS: one type of tangle net is made of fine twisted nylon twine and is used mainly for catching soles, plaice and flounder; another of heavier twine mainly for catching skates and rays. Typical of the former is a 127 mm mesh net 46 m long by 2.7 m deep set in by the half and so mounted as to fish 1.2 m deep. Typical of the latter is a 430 mm mesh net 110 m long set in by the half and so mounted as to fish 2 m deep. It will catch crawfish, turbot, monk and other large fish as well as skates and rays. It is often known as a RAY NET.

TRAMMEL NETS: tangle nets consisting of one inner wall of 76–126 mm mesh netting and two outer walls of 460 mm mesh netting. Inner walls are set in by the half and are twice the depth of outer walls so that they hang loosely and there is plenty of slack to be carried through the latter. These nets are usually moored and will tangle most species of fish.

TRAWLS: conical-shaped nets which are towed along the seabed by single vessels to catch demersal fish, shrimps and prawns; or towed between seabed and surface by one or two vessels to catch pelagic fish. Mouths are held open by beams or otter boards.

WRECK NETS: tangle nets made of twisted multifilament, monofilament or multi-monofilament nylon. About sixty metres long on the headline, eighty metres long on the footline, they are set in 4:1 or so and are fitted with iron rings at foot. Used to tangle cod, pollack etc. over and around wrecks.

All these types of net are made and often stocked by leading netmakers. Nets such as FLUE (PETER, SPLASH or BEATING) NETS for catching flat fish; PUSH NETS for catching shrimps; STAKE (BAULK, STREAM, BAG or KEDDLE) NETS for setting on beaches and banks to catch a variety of species; and TROUSER (TWIN TAILED) TRAWLS for manual hauling are made by specialist netmakers.

Beach Seines, Draw and Draft Nets

'Are draw and drift nets made and worked in the same way as beach seine nets? If, not, can you tell us what the difference is between them?'

Draw nets and beach seines are identical in the way they are made and worked but a draft net is a somewhat special kind of beach seine.

The former are made in various sizes and in various mesh sizes. They are used to capture a variety of species but the method of working them is the same.

The net is stowed in the stern of a small boat and a warp attached to one end of it is held by a man on the beach while his mate rows round in a semicircle before landing with a warp attached to the other end of the net further along the beach. Both then haul away steadily to draw all fish gilled or encircled by the net on to the beach.

Draft nets, as used on the Dee in Cheshire and possibly elsewhere for catching salmon, are gill nets between 170 and 200 metres long – usually made of nylon nowadays.

The main body of a draft net, which has a bag in the middle of it, is made of 102 mm mesh nylon twine forty-five meshes deep and the wings or gales of 127 mm mesh, thirty-five meshes deep. Top of the net is attached to a 25 mm circumference line with floats on it and the bottom to a leadline. A large float is secured to the top of the bag and draft ropes are attached to the wings of the net.

Draft nets are usually worked from sandbanks in the estuary. Procedure is for one man to row out at right angles from a bank on either flood or ebb in a boat about five metres long and then turn and shoot the net with the stream. His mate meanwhile remains at the point of launching holding on to one draft rope.

When the boatman has shot the net, he rows as directly as possible into the bank, paying out his draft rope. When he lands, he may be one hundred metres or so away from his mate.

Having landed, he hauls in his wing-end of the net. And when he has done so, his mate starts to walk along the bank towards him until only a distance of about ten metres separates them.

Then both start hauling together, edging gradually towards each other as the net comes in. While hauling, care is taken to ensure that the float-marked bag is middled all the time.

Creepers – Greepers

'I have always used a grapnel to recover lost gear but recently I have lost two grapnels and quite a lot of line due to their getting fast among rocks. I understand that there are devices called creepers or greepers, designed and constructed specifically for recovering gear, which are not as likely to get snagged in rough ground as grapnels. If you know anything about them, will you please send me as much information as you can?'

You could, if you can spare the time, make a type of grapnel which is not likely to become as irretrievable in rocks as an ordinary one although equally effective for recovering gear.

All you need to do so is about a metre of 50mm interior diameter steel piping and two lengths of steel rod about 9mm in diameter. You bend each rod double and push it through the piping until about 76mm of the double part protrudes from the far end. You then open the protrusions to form an eye to which a rope can be attached and bend back the four single ends of rod at the other end of the piping at an equal distance apart to form four barbless anchor arms. This type of grapnel is inexpensive to make and has the merit that if it gets caught in rocks when grappling gear, the arms will straighten and allow it to be retrieved.

A type of creeper which you can make yourself consists of a length of chain with about half a dozen shark hooks attached to it in bunches at intervals of 460mm. It is suitable for recovering lines from all except rocky bottom and likely to be more effective than a grapnel for the purpose.

If neither of these devices appeals to you, you could probably get your local blacksmith to make you a type of creeper favoured by some lobster fishermen. It consists of an iron shaft about a metre long with an eye and a ring through it at one end and five barbed arms bent back for about 150mm at the other. A merit about this one is that it can be used not only for retrieving lost gear but, when working close in to rocks, for anchoring a small boat temporarily or hauling off in the event of an engine stoppage. Being fairly light, it can be thrown a useful distance.

There are two types of creeper made by manufacturers of fishing gear. One consists of a stout steel bar a metre long which weighs 20kg. It has a 32mm eye in one end and, welded to it at an acute angle at intervals along its length, ten 16mm diameter steel spikes. This type of creeper is sometimes made in two lengths, each about 460mm long, shackled together.

The other is made of two 460mm lengths of 100x100x6mm angle iron, joined back to back, with five slots cut into each of the four sides and an eye welded on to both ends. Two such lengths, joined by 460mm of chain, form a complete creeper, the eye in the end of the second one being used to attach a trip line.

To catch Skates and Rays

'Thornback Ray, locally called Roker, and maybe Skate come close in here in spring and autumn. Can you tell me as much about these fish as possible and say which you think would be the best way for me to catch them?'

The Common Skate grows to a larger size than the Roker – up to two metres across the back and fins and over 100kg in weight – and generally has a longer nose than a roker of equivalent size. Its back is grey shading to mauve at the wing tips and its belly is grey-blue with spots on it.

The roker's back is a mottled grey-brown and its belly is white without any spots on it. The male roker is easy to identify by four rows of hooked denticles on its back – denticles which originally caused it to be called Thornback Ray.

You could catch both species with a longline if you can obtain fresh herring, mackerel, pilchards or sprats for bait. But you might find yourself in trouble if a big fish were to get hooked. I therefore think that the most feasible way for you to do so would be to use a beam trawl.

To catch and cook Brown Shrimps

'Could you tell me how to catch brown shrimps and how to cook them on board?'

Brown shrimps (*Crangon crangon* or *Crangon vulgaris*) are found on sand or mud bottom, and not infrequently along edges (boundaries between hard and mud bottom) in shallow water.

Best procedure to catch the comparatively small quantities you are likely to want would be to get a beam fish trawl, of a size which you can handle easily, with a detachable cod-end and also a cod-end made of shrimp netting. So equipped you would be able to use the trawl both for catching flat fish and for catching shrimps. Towing speed is the same whichever you are after.

First job after hauling and releasing the catch from the cod-end is to sort edible shrimps from small ones, immature flat fish and rubbish. Then it's best to wash the former and cook them as soon as possible.

You use sea water in the boiler and ensure that it is boiling before you start putting batches of shrimps into it. If the water is kept on the boil and a ratio of about a kilo of shrimps to five litres of water is maintained, six or seven minutes is sufficient to cook each batch. After cooking they should be cooled over the side or on a sheet of canvas.

To Catch Grey Mullet

'Can you tell me anything about grey mullet and how to catch them?'

Grey mullet enter estuaries and rivers in spring and early summer and return to the sea about the time that first frosts occur in autumn. They feed on small organisms to be found in weed; also by scraping mud bottom and extracting decomposing vegetable matter. They grow to a weight of four or five kilos but you are seldom likely to catch any weighing much more than two kilos.

They can be speared and caught with handlines but in most places are only taken with trammel, gill and beach seine nets.

If there is not much weed about, you can take mullet in large quantities in trammel nets and at the same time tangle a few bass. You can set them across creeks which run into estuaries and leave them down all night but if you do so, there may be a lot of jellyfish and rubbish as well as mullet in them when you haul.

Clearing a trammel can be a laborious and time-wasting business and you may find it more satisfactory to set one across a creek when the ebb tide starts to slacken about an hour and a half before low water and to haul it before the flood starts to flow with any strength an hour or two after low water.

If there is much weed about and jellyfish are carried backwards and forwards by tidal streams, you would be likely to find it more satisfactory to use a gill net – a 76 mm mesh net early in the season, a 102 mm mesh net later on. You set such a net in the same places and at the same times as you would a trammel or, as it would be designed to fish close to the surface instead of on the bottom, you could let it drift athwart the tide instead of mooring it.

To Hook Herring

'I have always been under the impression that herring feed principally on plankton and that, for this reason, it is not possible to catch them with hook and line. But I was told the other day that adult herring eat shrimps, sand eels and whitebait, and that it is possible to catch them with baited – and even bare – hooks under suitable conditions when they rise towards the surface around dusk. If this is a fact, can you give me any information about how hooks should be rigged and worked?'

Herring are sometimes taken with baited hooks in winter off the coasts of Devon and Cornwall. Tackle used consists of three short-shanked, size 10 hooks, suspended on a trace and two droppers below a few split shot and a light float. This arrangement is attached to monofilament nylon line with a breaking strength of about 1.5 kg.

Ragworms about 76 mm long are used for bait. Each is threaded on a hook so that one half covers it except for barb and point, and the other half dangles free. With hooks so baited, herring are caught when they swim into brightly lit harbours towards high water. Roach rods about three metres long have proved as effective as any for working the tackle.

When herring appear off the coast of Antrim in Northern Ireland in spring, they will take bare hooks with enthusiasm. One successful fisherman there uses a rod with a fixed spool reel, a monofilament nylon line with a

283 gm sinker on the end of it and six No. 16 clean, bare haddock hooks set 38 mm off it at 230 mm intervals. He requires his rods to be able to withstand a seasonal strain of half a tonne of herrings!

The shoals from which he makes his catch are said to enter the North Channel around March, some of their number having been caught in Rathlin Sound and off Fair Head in the early part of the year. They reach the vicinity of Hunter Rock and The Maidens between early April and the middle of May, and on arrival off Islandmagee are in poor condition and entirely devoid of fat. By the middle of June they are in prime condition and are mostly caught with bare hooks on jigs.

The traditional jig is an oval-shaped lead weighing a little over a kilo with a triple hook at the bottom end and a pair of hooks attached to short droppers threaded through it in a similar way to that in which hooks are attached to a Scottish cod ripper.

Expert jiggers, whose boats have a beam of two to three metres, rig as many as five bars on eighteen metre main lines and attach 1 kg lead sinkers or 'murderers' at the lower end. They do not take each fish off the hook by hand but jerk the catch into the bottom of the boat and the jig back over the side again. When shoals are at a depth of 6–12 m, average catch of jiggers using five bars is about four hundred fish a night.

For over one hundred years there has been a substantial bare hook jig fishery off the Antrim coast from early in May to about the end of June. Some four hundred jiggers customarily take part in it to provide their families with fresh, salted, smoked and frozen herring.

According to one experienced participant in the fishery, they will take bare hooks when feeding on fry. They can only be caught in quantity from sunset to dusk and are seldom caught during the day. Ideal conditions are a warm, calm evening when the fish start rising at sundown to a depth of about twelve metres and later to a depth of six metres as the light fades. If they are hooked at greater depths than these, they are likely to be lost on account of their soft mouths.

The traditional jig has been improved upon by development of a jig incorporating a number of 'bars'. A bar consists of two 460 mm lengths of piano wire twisted together so that two individual 90 mm lengths of wire protrude at either end in the shape of a V. To the ends of the individual wires are attached 40 mm droppers and to these are attached bright new No. 10 haddock hooks. Distance between pairs of hooks is about 300 mm.

An islander who has hooked herring around Islandmagee for over fifty years, not so long ago provided me with information about them which might be of value to you. He said that they are not worth catching until they can be fried in their own fat.

To Smoke Surplus Catches

'In the summer we sometimes catch more mackerel, in winter more whiting than we want for immediate consumption. So we are thinking of making smoking apparatus to process surplus catches. Can you tell us what is involved in curing and smoking these and other species such as herring, and cod, and let us know how we can make a smoker to process small quantities?'

Since the species you mention have to be salt cured before they are smoked, first involvement is acquisition of salt suitable for the purpose. Best for brining prior to smoking is vacuum dried salt – table salt as used domestically for seasoning. This can be bought in bulk quantities from wholesale grocers.

Coarser grades of salt, known by such names as fishery, country or rock salt, are sometimes used for fish processing but impurities in them occasionally cause imperfect smoked products. Defects are usually visual, perhaps white crystals forming on the surface of the fish, or discoloration.

Having obtained the right kind of salt, the next thing to do is to prepare a brine solution. Some use a solution consisting of 6 kg of salt dissolved in thirty-six litres of water for every 50 kg of fish; others a solution in which a potato will float.

Usual way to prepare fish for brining and smoking is to remove heads and guts and then split them in the same way as herring are split for kippering. If they are larger than average, parts of backbones are removed and slits made to allow salt to penetrate. They are then scrubbed in fresh water with a brush to remove all remains of blood, guts and unwanted tissue.

Thereafter they are steeped in the brine for 30–90 minutes before being removed and strung up in the shade to drip and drain. They are ready to smoke when they become tacky.

Fish can be either cold smoked in smoke at a temperature of less than 30°C or hot smoked in smoke at a higher temperature. Object of the former process is to dry and flavour them; of the latter to cook and flavour them.

Procedure and lengths of time they are left in smoke vary according to type of smokehouse, pit or apparatus used. Simplest smoking device of all is a 180 litre drum with both ends removed, placed upright on flat stones so that its lower rim is about 25 mm off the ground all round. Procedure when this contrivance is used will give you some idea of what is involved in the actual smoking process.

Drill in this case is to place inside it on the ground a baking dish filled with sawdust (preferably oak) and wood chips, and then to start the contents smoking by placing a glowing ember in them. When the smoke becomes dense the fish are placed on spits across the top end of the drum and covered by a fish box or basket upside down. The latter is then covered with a sack to keep in most but not all of the smoke so that the fish do not get overheated and drop off the spits.

They are best kept in the smoke for six or seven hours, sawdust being replenished as required to maintain an adequate quantity and density of smoke. They are removed when they have become an attractive golden brown colour and hung where they are surrounded by clean, cool air until they are firm and cold.

To Shoot Seals Legally

'A seal took a great interest in proceedings when we shot a drift net the other evening, an interest which increased when we fixed a flashing light to one end of it. It surfaced near the light and inspected it; then dived under it and swam at high speed along the length of the net. Thereafter it gambolled around, apparently anticipating a supper of fresh herring. We managed to frighten it away before there were any to eat but its presence posed two questions: what kind of seal was it likely to have been and would it have been legally permissible for one of us to shoot it with a 12-bore shotgun loaded with cartridges filled with No. 4 shot? We should be greatly obliged if you could answer them.'

It was probably a Common Seal, possibly a Grey Seal.

Common Seals are constant residents in all suitable localities around the English, Scottish and Irish coasts. Although the most secluded and out-of-the-way havens are selected as their habitual dwelling places, there are few localities where they may not occasionally be seen. They frequent bays, inlets and estuaries and are usually to be seen on sandbanks or mud flats which dry at low water.

The young are born at the end of May or beginning of June. They feed chiefly on fish, being particularly fond of salmon. They grow to a length of 1.5 m and are usually a yellowish grey colour with irregular spots of dark brown or black above and yellowish white beneath.

The Grey Seal grows to a larger size, adult males often attaining a length of 2.4 m. The form of its skull and the simple character of its molar teeth distinguish it from the Common Seal. It is a yellowish grey colour, lighter beneath, with dark grey spots or blotches. It is, however, like most other seals, liable to great variations of colour according to age. It is not migratory and is seldom encountered far from land. Its favourite breeding places are rocky islets, its young being born towards the end of September or in October or November.

Adult Grey Seals are recognisable, when they rear their heads out of the water by four or five rings of hair a little longer than that of the rest of the body. This makes them look as though they have several rings of rope around their necks.

It would not have been legally permissible for you to have killed the seal with a shotgun. Part 1 of the Conservation of Seals Act 1970 states that any person, who uses for the purpose of killing or taking any seal, any poisonous substance or uses for the purpose of killing, injuring or taking and seal any firearm OTHER THAN A RIFLE using ammunition having a muzzle energy of not less than six hundred footpounds and a bullet weighing not less than sixty grains shall be guilty of an offence.

As you did not know what species of seal it was, you could have contravened the law by killing it even with an approved type of rifle as there are close seasons for shooting seals. There is an annual close season for Common Seals (*Phoca vitulina*) from 1st June to 31st August and for Grey Seals (*Halichoerus grypus*) from 1st September to 31st December inclusive.

It may interest you, in case you should be in a quandary about killing seals in future, to know that a person shall not be guilty of an offence under Section 2 or 3 of the Act by reason only of the killing or attempted killing of any seal to prevent it from causing damage to a fishing net or fishing tackle in his possession...or to any fish for the time being in such fishing net, provided that at the time the seal was in the vicinity of such net or tackle.

Soft Crabs for Bait

'I have been told that soft crabs make good bait for hooking cod and whiting. As lugworms are hard to come by here – except at a diabolical price – I would like to try using crabs. I would appreciate any information you can send me about them – particularly where to find them.'

Soft crabs most commonly found are Common or Shore Crabs (*Carcinus moenas*) which are about to moult or have recently moulted. Sometimes they are small edible crabs (*Cancer pagurus*). They are to be found anywhere around the coast where there are plenty of rocks and/or stones.

Common or Shore crabs are a greenish colour and each has four pairs of legs and two pincers. Males can be recognised by their large pincers and a narrow apron on the underside; females by their comparatively small pincers and a wide, dark coloured apron.

Like all crustaceans, crabs have to discard their hard, protective shell covering from time to time and grow another one. They generally undergo this moulting process during the summer, having previously grown underneath their shells a soft, tough skin which covers all parts of the body.

As the time for moulting approaches, they cease to feed and retire to pools in which seaweed or stones afford them protective cover.

At this stage male crabs are sometimes known as peeler crabs as their shells can be peeled off the soft skin inside to yield ideal bait. To find out whether one is suitable for bait, you break off the outer tip of one of the legs and if a dark red skin protrudes you can take it that moulting time is near. You then pull off legs and pincers, strip the shell firstly from the underside and secondly from the back, and you should have a crab with an unbroken soft skin.

After retiring to a pool, the shell of a male crab which is left undisturbed cracks in due course and the crab emerges from it covered only by the soft skin. This takes about five weeks to harden, during most of which time the crab is suitable for bait.

As a female crab approaches moulting time, it seeks the protection of an old male crab. The latter enfolds it and contiues to embrace it until it has moulted and grown a new hard shell. If you find a female crab in the embrace of a large male crab, it is almost certain that it will be suitable for bait.

If you should find a peeler or soft crab and are in any doubt whether it is a common crab or an edible one, it would be best not to use it for bait.

Several years ago the Eastern Sea Fisheries Joint Committee made a by-law prohibiting the use of any edible crab whatever its size or condition, or any part of such crab, for bait. And the Sea Fisheries Committee for your district may have done the same.

Whether it has or has not, it clearly makes sense not to use small crabs which will become edible, for bait.

Sea Horses and Pipe Fishes

'Just look at this. What on earth is it? – a Sea Horse or what?'

He held up a weird little fish about 300 mm long which looked as though both its head and its body had been forcibly stretched. Its mouth was circular, unlike that of any other species.

It wasn't a Sea Horse, which is easily distinguishable by its horse-like head, but either a Great or Broad-nosed Pipe Fish. These are both frequenters of inshore waters all round the British Isles whereas Sea Horses are mostly to be found on the South Coast of England and around the Cornish coast.

Great and Broad-nosed pipe fishes are members of the same family as Sea Horses and there are also three other members of it – Snake, Worm and Straight-nosed pipe fishes. The bodies of all except the Sea Horse are encased in a series of jointed bony rings which form a flexible armour and the abdomens of the females have a pouch which serves as a refuge for young fry just as the pouch of a female kangaroo does for her joey.

Pipe fishes generally cruise along slowly in a vertical position and, like Sea Horses, sometimes moor themselves with their prehensile tails around seaweed. But, if necessary, they can move horizontally and rapidly like eels.

Their food consists almost exclusively of tiny crustaceans and they use their long snouts to poke into clumps of weed after them.

Great pipe fishes grow to a length of 460mm and the Broad-nosed variety to 330mm. The little flesh on them is said to be not impalatable when cooked.

Sparling

'I saw in a recent report that a Sea Fisheries Committee patrol boat had made several attempts to catch sparling for experimental purposes, without success. Could you please tell me what a sparling is?'

Sparling is an alternative name for Smelt (*Osmerus eperlanus*) which are usually caught close inshore and in estuaries where they spawn in spring.

The European smelt, which is remarkable for smelling like a cucumber, is good to eat but is seldom, if ever, sufficiently abundant to be caught in large numbers.

The Sea Lamphrey

'Have you any suggestions as to the identity of a ferocious little fish which attacked a friend of mine when he was swimming in Broadstairs Bay in Kent in three metres of water about fifty metres offshore recently? He tells me that he felt a sharp pain in his chest and saw that a small fish about the size of a mature sprat had attached itself with what appeared to be fangs. He tore it off, losing some flesh in the process, and crushed the life out of it. Although the wound bled freely, he experienced dizziness and double vision shortly after reaching the shore and he was treated in hospital for blood poisoning.'

I guess it was a small Sea Lamphrey, an eel-like species which grows to a length of about a metre and is remarkable for the sucker it uses instead of a mouth.

The sucker consists of a more or less circular suctorial lip surrounded by some weirdly arranged teeth. There are two maxillary teeth set close together; the tooth of the lower jaw is crescent-shaped and has about eight cusps; on the tongue there are four ridged teeth placed in pairs; and on the inner side of the suctorial disc there are about eight rows of sharp teeth, called suctorial teeth.

By means of the suctorial disc the lamphrey can attach itself very firmly to another fish and its teeth are ideally constructed for rasping chunks of flesh from its victim. This is its usual method of feeding. In the case of your friend, one might have fancied a change of diet.

Kippers, Bloaters etc.

'What exactly is the difference between a kipper, a bloater and a buckling?'

Kippers are produced by cold smoking fat herrings which have been gutted, split down the back, lightly brined and perhaps dyed. The smoking temperature does not exceed 30°C and the smoking process takes about four hours in a mechanical kiln.

Bloaters are whole, ungutted herring which have been dry salted for about six hours and cold smoked for eight to twelve hours in a chimney kiln or four hours in a mechanical kiln. While in a kiln they are dried for most of the time without smoke, which is only applied during the last hour or so; they thus retain their bright silver appearance.

Buckling are produced by first of all 'nobbing' herring – removing the head and long gut. When this has been done they are brined and hot smoked for about three hours in a mechanical kiln, the flesh being cooked during the process. They are relished more in the UK than red herring which are produced by heavily salting whole, ungutted herring and then cold smoking them for two or three weeks. The latter are mostly exported.

How to Souse Herrings

'I am getting a few herrings in my trammel net just now and I would like to try sousing them. Do you happen to know how to do it?'

The best soused herrings I have ever eaten were produced by using one of Madame Prunier's recipes. She recommends that you take about twenty herrings, clean them and cook them in a marinade.

The marinade consists of 600 ml of vinegar, 20 gm of salt, a litre of white wine, two medium-sized carrots cut in thin rings, three medium-sized onions cut in thin rings, three minced shallots, a sprig of thyme and half a bay leaf, a pinch each of sage and basil, parsley stalks and several peppercorns.

Cooking consists of boiling the marinade gently until the carrot and onion are cooked, pouring it over the herrings arranged in a shallow pan and poaching them for twelve minutes without letting the liquid come to the boil.

After cooking you put them in a dish, pour the marinade over them and let them get cold. Then they are ready for consumption together, of course, with the marinade.

Another method of sousing them is to clean them, put them in a fire-proof dish with bay leaves, shredded onion, peppercorns, chillies and a sprinkling of salt, then cover them with equal parts of vinegar and water.

If they are large herrings, you then cook them for thirty minutes in a medium oven; if small for twenty minutes, after which you let them cool in the liquor before eating.

Nomenclature

'Whenever a French fisherman starts talking about langoustes, langoustines and écrevisses, I can't follow him. Is a langouste a lobster and, if so, what on earth is a langoustine?'

The French for lobster (*Homarus vulgaris*) is not langouste but Homard. Langouste means a sea-water crawfish (*Balinurus vulgaris*) and langoustine a Dublin Bay prawn or Norway Lobster (*Nephrops norvegicus*).

Écrevisses are fresh water crayfish which are found in many streams inland.

Your question reminds me of one posed by a Norwegian a little while ago. He was not sure about the English equivalent of sild, brisling and sardines.

Sild are herring (*Clupea harengus*), Brisling are sprats (*Clupea sprattus*) and Sardines are small pilchards (*Clupea pilchardus*).

Bioluminescence

'I should be grateful for any information you can let me have about fluorescence or "fire" in the sea at night. What causes it? Does the weather have anything to do with it? Is it worse at certain times of the year? Have the moon or static electricity anything to do with it? And is there any way of preventing it illuminating nets?'

What you call fluorescence was, until recently, generally known as phosphorescence because it used to be thought that it was caused by particles of phosphorus in the water. But since it was discovered that it is caused by plant and animal life, it has been known as bioluminescence.

According to information in *The Mariner's Handbook*, published by the Hydrographer of the Navy, it is caused by a variety of organisms, from microscopic marine life to many forms of deep-sea fish. Its production is attributed to biochemical reactions which, though apparently automatic in lower forms of life, are under nervous hormonal control in higher forms.

Research has shown that it may occur anywhere, but that it is encountered most frequently in warmer tropical seas. In the Arabian Sea it reaches a maximum in August. In some parts of the North Atlantic it reaches a maximum in summer; in others during spring.

A number of different types of the phenomenon are at present recognised. Among them are flashing patches; patches apparently expanding and contracting; disturbed water luminescence – in breaking waves or water disturbed by propellers or fishing nets; light-stimulated luminescence – possibly moonlight; and discrete blobs or shapes as from large creatures – presumably large fish disturbing water.

You could doubtless reduce luminescence caused by a revolving propeller by reducing revolutions and that caused by a towed net by towing it more slowly. But obviously you can't exercise any control over it when it is caused by a shoal of fish or a large fish disturbing the water, breaking waves etc.

If you want further information on the subject, you will find it in *The Marine Observer's Handbook*, which is published for the Meteorological Office by Her Majesty's Stationery Office and is obtainable through booksellers.

Jerseys and Guernseys

'What is the difference between jerseys and guernseys? Has it anything to do with length or colour, or whether patterns are knitted into them or not?'

If the names are used correctly, they refer to garments made in the respective Channel Islands exclusively. There is little difference in the length of island-made garments; they are both longer than the average pullover. And, although most are knitted with navy blue wool, both are made with natural, red, green or mustard coloured wool as well.

The main differences are in the hems and on the fronts. The hems of jerseys are ribbed and those of guernseys are moss-stitched. Designs are knitted into the fronts of jerseys but the fronts of guernseys are plain.

Traditional jerseys bear the parish emblem of the wearer worked into the front in a shield surround – to protect him against the perils of the sea. They became popular with fishermen who engaged in the Newfoundland fisheries from 1600 onwards as they were not only warm and hard wearing but indicated which of Jersey's twelve parishes the wearer came from.

Fishermen of other nationalities working the banks off Newfoundland noted and admired the jerseys and guernseys the Channel Islanders wore. And they presumably acquired samples to take home for copying; with the result that so-called garments began to be knitted in fishing ports everywhere, not invariably in conformity with traditional designs.

Patterns began to be knitted into guernseys to indicate the wearer's family and/or village. He could then be identified afloat or in a strange port as surely as could the wearer of a jersey with his parish emblem on the front. There was an additional advantage to be gained by departing from traditional design in this way; if he should happen to be lost overboard, those finding his body still clad in the guernsey could locate his relatives almost as easily as if he had been wearing an identity disc.

In the West Country and in Ireland, I believe, other variations from traditional designs were made. Young fishermen's girlfriends used to knit them guernseys with elaborate patterns indicating their romantic leanings in the hope that they would wear them as their 'bridal shirts' on their joint wedding day. These knitted love letters, intelligible during courtship only to the two lovers, were intermingled with more conventional cable, herringbone or other stitched patterns so that they could not be interpreted by others.

Pullovers like these are hybrids, liable to be called either jerseys or guernseys although they bear little resemblance in design to traditional island-made garments of either kind.

Spruce Boats

'I am looking for a boat suitable for line and lobster fishing – an open boat about five metres long which can be powered by an outboard engine. I am inclined towards buying one of a range of boats which are clinker-built of softwood in Norway. Do you know anything about them and, if so, would you recommend me to get one? I would also like to know whether I could tow a small beam trawl with such a boat.'

I know a little about them because I have used one as a tender and net boat for over ten years. As a consequence I can strongly recommend you to get one if you will be able to look after it in the way it was designed to be maintained.

The boats are planked with spruce grown in the north of Norway, or Sweden, on oak frames. Knees, gunwhales and rubbing strakes (if any) are of oak and fastenings are either copper or Swedish steel. An unusual feature in their construction – as they are clinker built – is that their seams are caulked. Another feature, not so unusual nowadays, is that they have stout transoms reinforced for outboard powering.

Their design is the result of developments over many centuries in building seaboats to enable inhabitants of North Norway to fish and to communicate. They are direct descendants of ten-oared Viking and Nordland boats and are consequently strong for their weight with lines which enable them to be driven easily by oars or engines.

If they are kept in the water most of the time and are only beached temporarily on occasion to land fish or load gear, as is probably the practice in Norway, their hulls will remain as watertight as you could wish. But leave them out of the water for more than a day or two in hot summer weather or cold, dry easterly winds in winter, and the planks may express resentment of such treatment by cracking longitudinally.

Using an outboard of adequate power, you would probably be able to work a trawl with a beam of up to three metres long successfully provided that you do not idle the engine too long and let it get overheated. It is advisable to maintain sufficient revolutions for the cooling water to circulate adequately and, if doing so entails towing too fast, add some chain to the groundrope.

'A designer and builder of boats was inspecting one on the slip here the other day and he said that vibration would be reduced if the deadwood were fined away. Can you tell me what causes vibration and whether steps other than fining away the deadwood can be taken to prevent it?'

Vibration can occur if the engine, even if properly installed and in good order, is unbalanced and pressure when a piston is moving down during the expansion stroke affects one engine bearer more than the other. This gives the engine a tendency to go out of alignment for a moment. It can occur if the propeller is unbalanced or mis-shapen, or if the stern tube does not project the right distance from the shaft log.

It can also occur if the shaft is misaligned, particularly if there are more than two bearings between engine and propeller. A shaft can become misaligned when a dry wooden boat is launched and assumes a slightly different shape in the water to that which it had when out of it. It will inevitably occur if a shaft is bent, too small or the engine beds are wrongly designed.

Therefore conventional ways of reducing vibration in a boat, other than fining away the deadwood, consist of checking the balance of the engine and the propeller, shape of propeller and length of sterntube, alignment of propeller shaft, design of engine beds and adjusting anything that is not as it should be.

Flexible couplings and flexible engine mountings are not infrequently used to minimise vibration but, since they have to transmit the thrust from the propeller, their effectiveness is limited because they cannot be soft enough.

As a consequence a device known as an Aquadrive, which allows considerable angular misalignment while accommodating axial movement, has been developed by a company in England. It incorporates a thrust bearing on the end of the propeller shaft to remove the thrust loading from the coupling and engine mounts.

This unit allows all parts of the joint to run at the same angular velocity while the engine is moving in all planes. It is therefore possible to use very soft mountings to isolate the engine from the hull of a boat, thus minimising vibration.

Angles of up to 16° may be obtained between the engine crankshaft and the propeller shaft. This makes it possible to install an engine horizontally or even below the line of the propeller shaft.

Not only does use of an Aquadrive unit minimise vibration in a boat but it has other advantages. Engine installation is simplified as there is no need to spend time aligning and re-aligning. A horizontal installation is considerably less expensive as regards fitting engine bearers. And height in an engine compartment can be saved, if required, by mounting an engine below the shaft line.

Laws and Regulations

'Presumably there are laws and regulations with which amateur as well as professional fishermen are supposed to comply. Would you please tell me where I can find out about those likely to affect me?'

Laws which might affect you have been enacted at the instance of such authorities as the Ministry of Agriculture, Fisheries and Food, the Department of Agriculture and Fisheries for Scotland, the Department of Agriculture for Northern Ireland and the Isle of Man Board of Agriculture and Fisheries. Fishery Officers employed by these authorities are stationed all around the coast for the purpose of enforcing them.

By-laws and regulations affecting coastal fishing in different districts have been made by Sea Fisheries Committees and regional Water Boards. And these authorities also employ Fishery officers to ensure as far as possible compliance with regulations.

Most of the laws and regulations likely to affect you are contained in Olsen's *Fisherman's Almanack*, published by E. T. W. Dennis and Sons Ltd, Scarborough. This is published annually and contains a wealth of information likely to be of value and interest to you.

It contains, for instance, regulations governing the minimum sizes of fish permitted to be landed and names and addresses of all Fishery Officers. The latter list could be of use to you should you ever wish to consult one about the legality of proposed operations.

CHAPTER FOUR

Sources of Supply

BOATS, GEAR AND EQUIPMENT

Boats

I have been asked from time to time what sort of boat I would recommend for fishing for the pot with lines, nets and traps. And I have usually replied that a boat similar to the one I have used for nearly thirty years could suit the inquirer admirably.

Osprey is clinker-built of larch on oak frames and is 9m overall with a beam of 2.6m and draught of 1.1m. She has a cabin forward, heated by a cooking range, in which two can camp in comfort. Aft of the cabin comes an engine room in which is installed a 22hp diesel engine and aft of that a well which provides plenty of space for stowing boatswain's stores and fishing gear.

The boat is equipped with mast and sails because I don't believe in going to sea without some alternative means of propulsion in the event of engine breakdown and because trolling under sail alone is a most effective and enjoyable method of catching some species of pelagic fish.

It would probably be prohibitively expensive to have a new boat built on similar lines nowadays. But smaller standard boats of not very different design, constructed of wood or glass reinforced plastic (GRP), are available and I think some are commendable.

One of them is known as the Jaunty. It can be constructed of wood or glass reinforced plastic and is 20ft (6m) overall with a beam of 7ft 9in (2.36m) and draught of just under 2ft (0.6m). It is equipped with a fore and mainsail, with a combined area of about 100sq.ft (9.29sq.m), and is powered by an 8hp diesel. The engine is installed at the fore end of a spacious well or cockpit in which an adequate amount of fishing gear can be stowed and worked.

The boat has a cabin forward in which two can cook, eat and sleep in comfort and plenty of stowage space for boatswain's stores etc. in a capacious locker at the after end of the well.

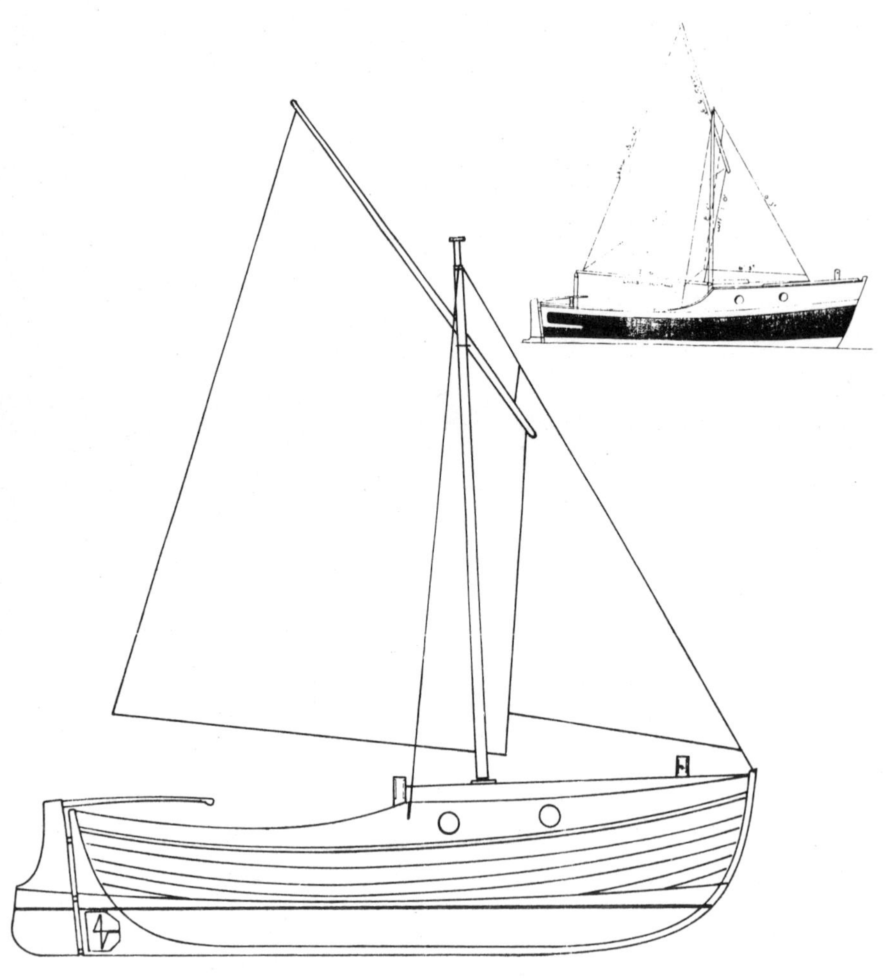

Gull 22   Jaunty 19/20

The other is known as the Gull 22. Designed, as was the Jaunty, by Peter Brown a partner of J. Francis Jones, Woodbridge, its length overall is 22ft (6.7m), beam 8ft 6in (2.6m) and draught just under 2ft (0.61m). It is designed on the lines of a traditional Norfolk clinker-built crabber.

It can be built of wood, if you are willing to pay a comparatively high price, but most Gulls constructed up to now have simulated clinker-built GRP hulls.

Everything about the Gull is simple, sturdy, robust and intended to

Cornish Crabber

withstand plenty of fair wear and tear. Its generous beam ensures a stable platform from which to work gear in most wind and sea conditions. Its 130 sq.ft (12 sq.m) lugsail is of adequate size to reach, run or troll under sail alone and its 10 hp diesel engine packs enough punch to tow a small trawl and to make satisfactory progress against all but abnormal winds and tides.

The cabin is large enough for a couple of bunks with sitting headroom and a heating/cooking stove. There is adequate space in the well to stow lines, a net or two and a collapsible beam trawl.

Both boats are economical to maintain and operate. Neither costs a fortune to insure. They are small enough to work single-handed but there is enough room in them for two to camp on board in comfort. They can be used in shoal water and will sit upright in the mud if grounded. Either will serve as a base for wildfowling operations if kept in saltings in winter.

For those who want to be able to sail to and from fishing grounds, the Elton Boatbuilding Company, Castledykes, Kircudbright can supply a suitable boat for handlining and trolling. It is clinker-built of wood and its length overall is 6 m, beam 2.3 m and draught 1.2 m (with centreboard down). (See opposite page.)

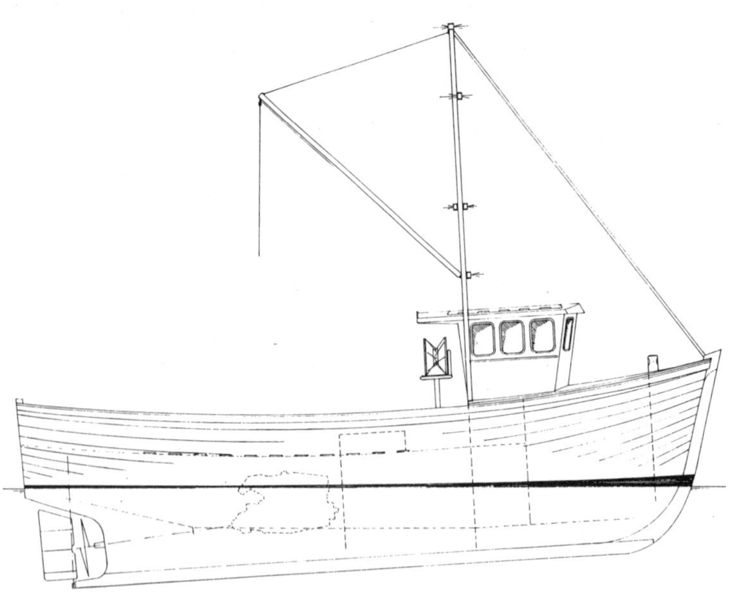

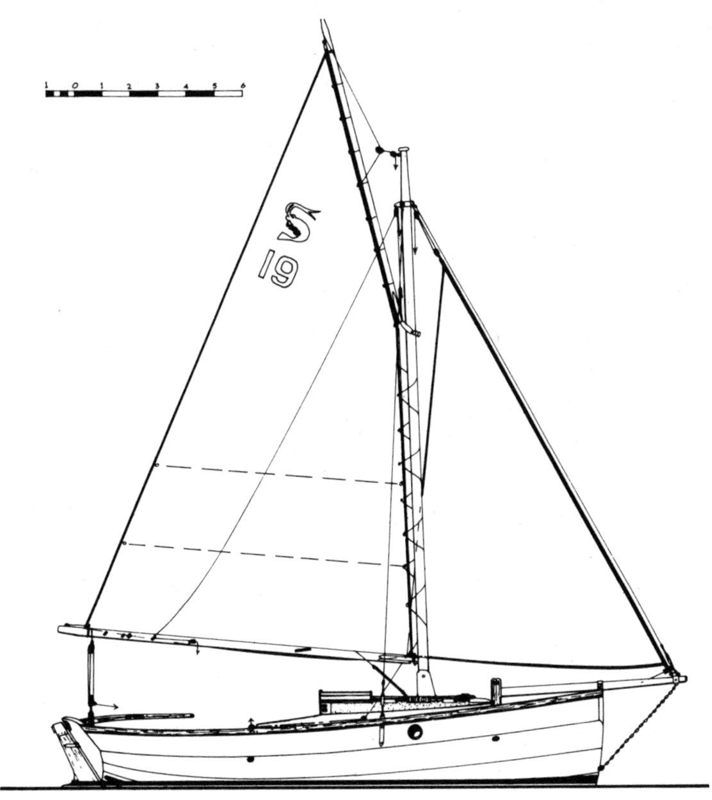

For those who don't want to be able to set any sail, the Elton Boatbuilding Company can supply a standard boat which can be used for any form of coastal fishing. It is clinker-built of wood and is 10.7 m overall with a beam of 4.1 m and draught of 1.5 m. (See opposite page.)

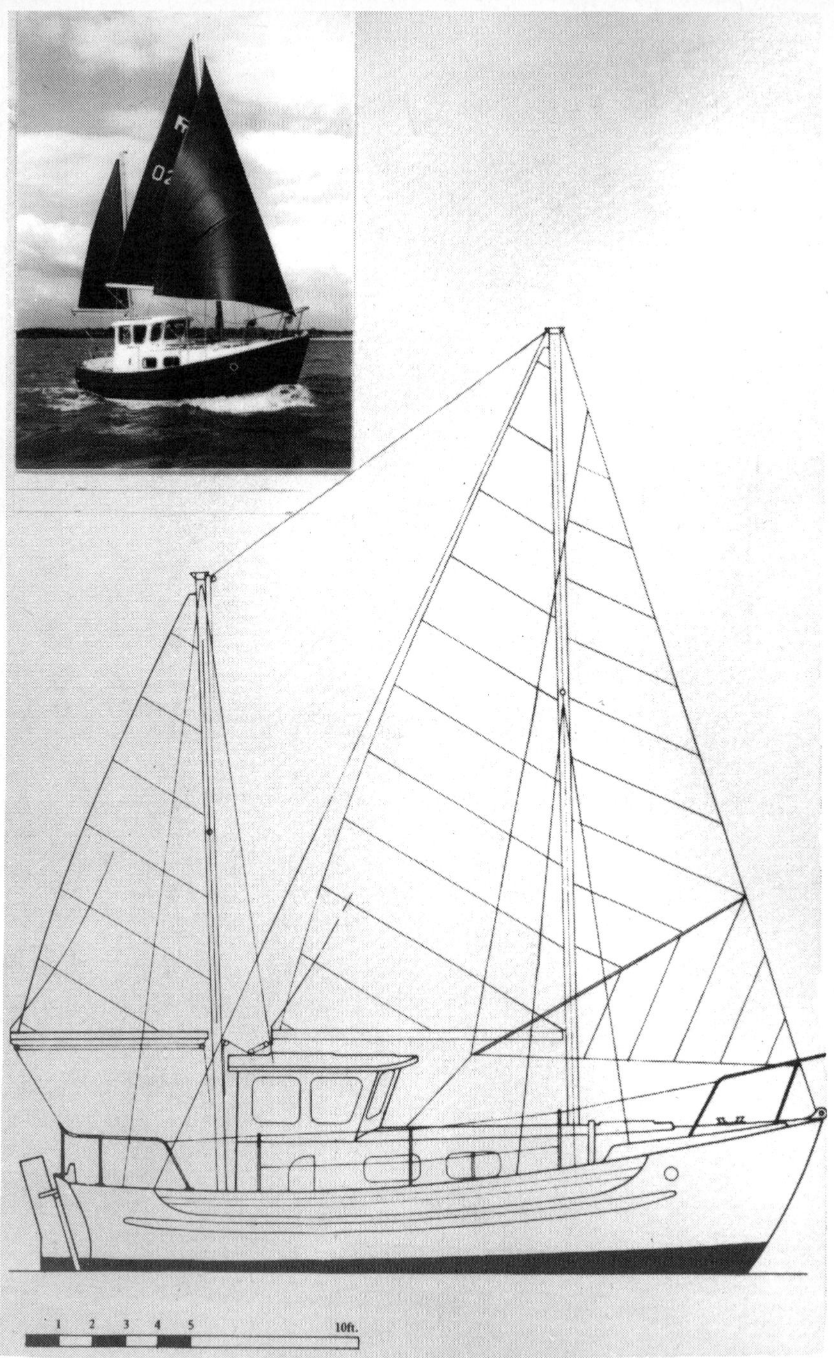

Fisher 25

Another sailing boat suitable for handlining and trolling is available from Cornish Crabbers Ltd, Rock, Wadebridge, Cornwall. It is known as the Cornish Shrimper, has a GRP hull and its dimensions are 5.8x2.1x1.2m (with centreboard down).

For those who want a boat with plenty of accommodation from which they can handline and troll, the 'Fisher 25' may be considered suitable. It measures 7.7 x 2.8 x 1.1m. Like other 'Fisher' boats of greater size, its hull is built of GRP by North Shore Yacht Yards Ltd, Itchenor Shipyard, Chichester, Sussex.

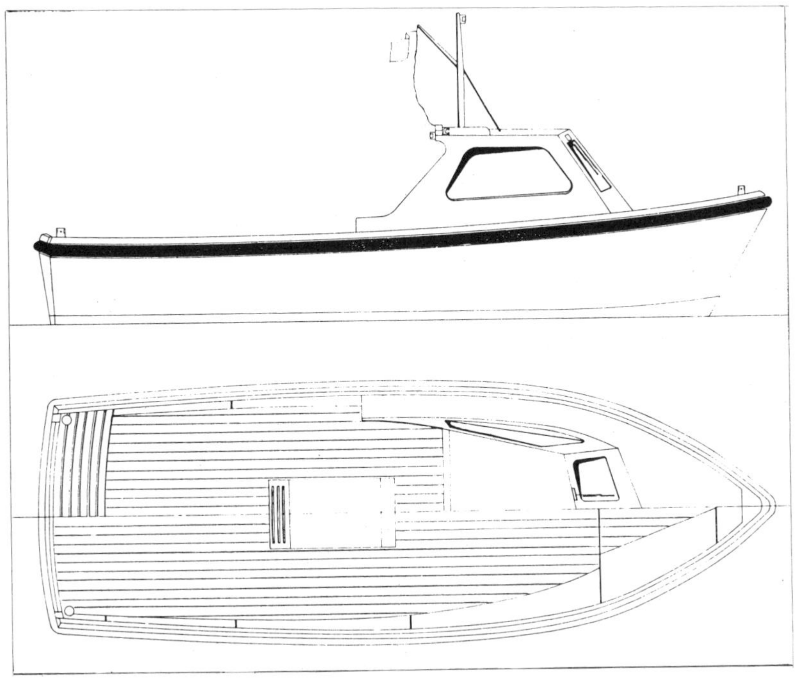

Versatility

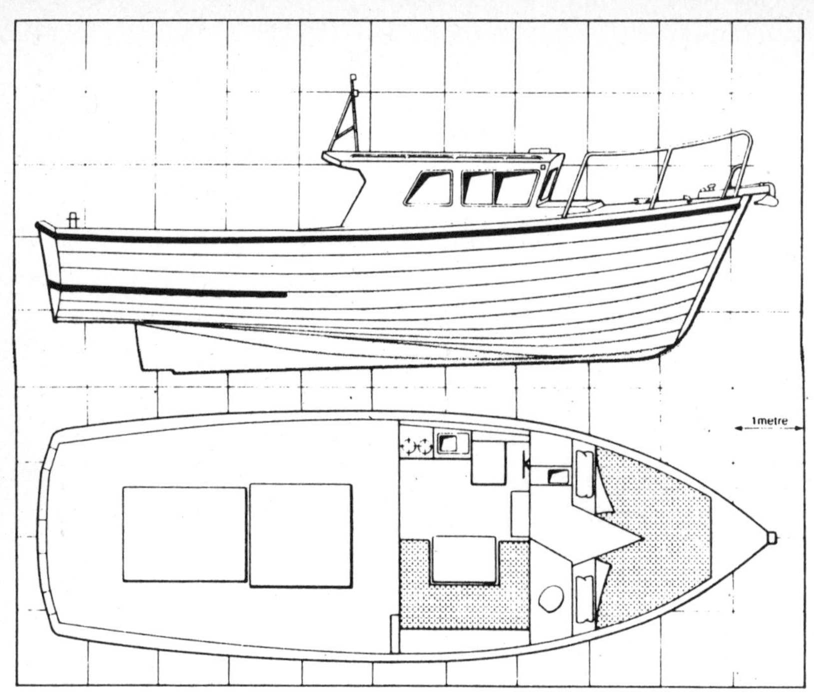

Starfish 10

Wasp

No less than three GRP boats suitable for fishing for the pot are produced by the Tyler Boat Company Ltd, at its premises in Morley Road, Tonbridge, Kent.

Fastest of them is the Wasp (pictured) which measures 8.31 x 2.82 x 0.69m. Then come the Versatility 30 and the Versatility 25. The former measures 9.22 x 3.27 x 1.07m – the latter 7.62 x 2.80 x 0.76m.

Fast GRP boats with plenty of accommodation are produced by Bounty Boats Ltd at Brundall, Norwich. They have been designed by Hugh Easton and are known as the Starfish 8 and the Starfish 10. The former is 8.15m overall with a beam of 2.90m and draught of 0.76m; the latter is 10.32 x 3.45 x 0.92m.

A handy little boat for inshore fishing is produced by Armada Marine Plastics Ltd, Carbeile Mill, Torpoint, Cornwall. It is known as the Tamar 2000 Fisherman and measures 7.16 x 2.59 x 0.71m. The standard version is fitted with a hydraulic pot hauler.

Tamar 2000 Fisherman

Duver 23

Mustang Marine Ltd, Clarence Boatyard, East Cowes, Isle of Wight can supply several boats designed for use by professional fishermen but they lack the accommodation likely to be required by those wanting to anchor near pots or nets which they have set to fish all night. More suitable for the latter is their Duver 23 which has comfortable accommodation. It is 7 m over all with a beam of 2.4 m and draught of 0.6 m.

If you intend to moor your boat at a considerable distance from your fishing grounds, you may prefer a boat capable of being driven at high speeds. In this case a Lochin 33, built of GRP by Lochin Marine (Rye) Ltd, Rock Channel, Rye, Sussex might suit you admirably. It is 10 m overall with a beam of 3.5 m and draws a little over 1 m. It can be driven at speeds up to 26 knots.

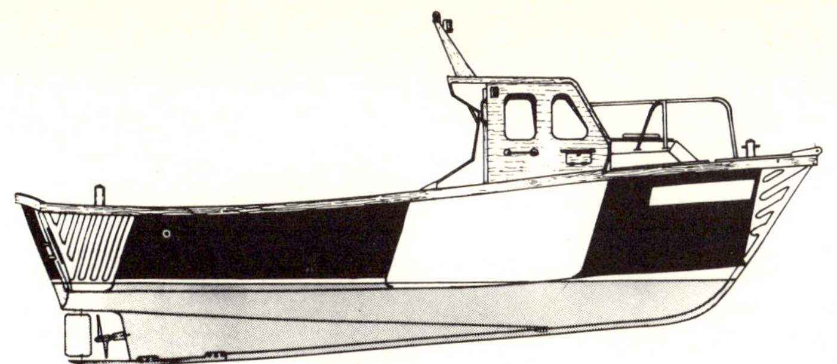

STARBOARD PROFILE

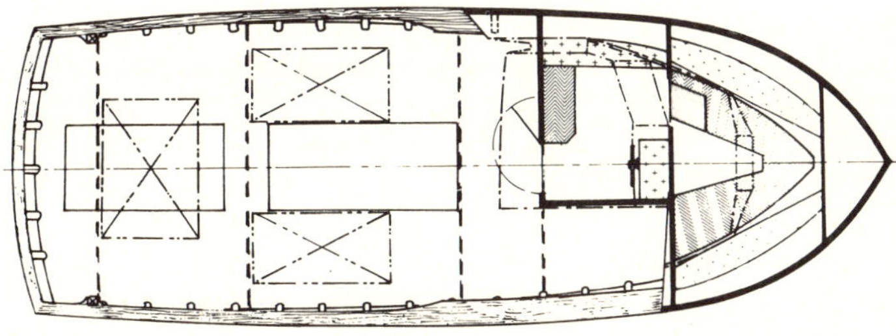

TYPICAL PLAN VIEW

Lochin 33 Rigged for potting and longlining

Should none of the boats described here suit your requirements exactly or if you have a mind to build your own boat with wood or steel, Naval Architect Denis Swire at Porthleven, Cornwall is likely to be able to help you. He could not only design a boat which would be just what you want but supply plans drawn up so that the construction method is clearly shown.

DS 20 General Arrangement Fishing Boat

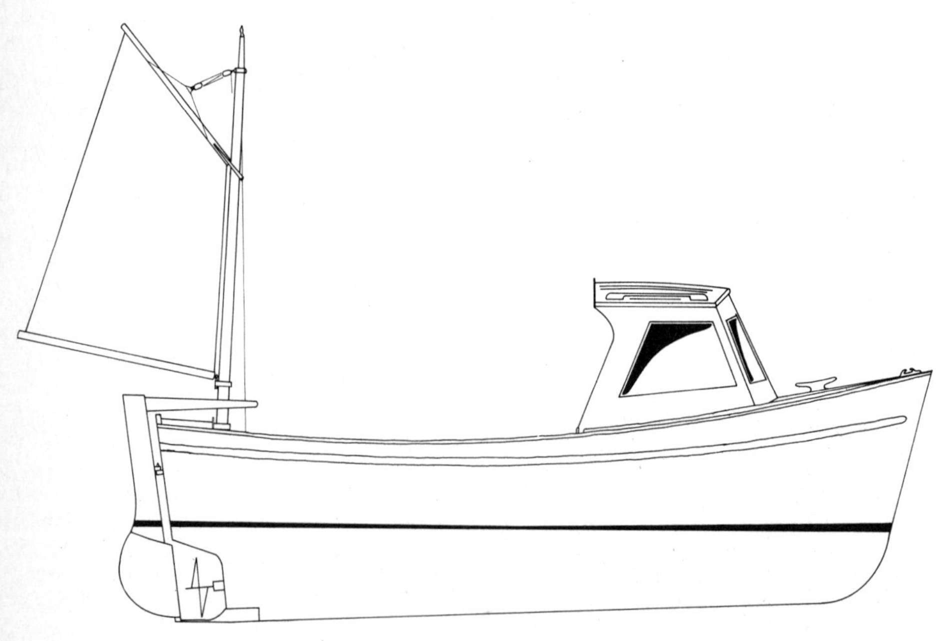

Gear and Equipment

Having acquired your boat it is possible that you may not know where to get some items of equipment you need to operate it or some items of fishing gear that you want to work from it.

Here, therefore, is a list of manufacturers and suppliers who will be able to provide all or any of your requirements.

I could make it much more extensive if I were to include scores of concerns which may or may not be in business in a year or two's time and more elaborate if I were to include telephone and telex numbers. But changes take place so rapidly nowadays that such a list would soon become out of date.

Those in this list are well-established concerns with most of whom I have had satisfactory dealings.

If it should happen that you can't get what you want from one or other of them, or want more information about sources of supply, your best procedure would be to buy a copy of *Fishing News* from AGB Heighway each week. In it you will find advertised the most up-to-date items of gear and equipment and the phone numbers of advertisers.

Almanack, Fisherman's: E.T.W.Dennis & Sons Ltd, Melrose Street, Scarborough, North Yorkshire YO12 7SJ.

Almanac, Nautical: Thomas Reed Publications Ltd, 178/185 High Street West, Sunderland.

Books about Fishing: Fishing News Book Ltd, Long Garden Walk, Farnham, Surrey.

Cathodic Protection Anodes: M.G.Duff Marine Ltd, Birdham, Chichester, Sussex PO20 7EW.

Chain and Components (Dragalloy): Wheway Watson (CM) Ltd, Green Lane, Walsall, West Midlands WS2 8HU.

Electrical Equipment: Lucas Marine Ltd, Frimley Road, Camberley, Surrey GU16 5EU.

Engines, new and reconditioned: T.Norris Industries Ltd, 6 Wood Lane, Isleworth, Middlesex TW7 5ER.

Engines, diesel and petrol: A.N.Weaver (Coventry Victor) Ltd, Smiths Industrial Estate, Humber Avenue, Coventry CV3 1JL.

Fishing Boat Designer: Denis Swire, C.Eng., FRINA, Sunset Gardens, Porthleven, Cornwall TR13 9BS.

Fishing Charts: Imray, Laurie, Norie and Wilson Ltd, Wych House, The Broadway, St Ives, Huntingdon, Cambridgeshire PE17 4BT.

Fishing Gear and Equipment: Bridport-Gundry Ltd, The Court, West Street, Bridport, Dorset DT6 3QU. (Branches in Brixham, Whitby, Musselburgh, Aberdeen and Killybegs).

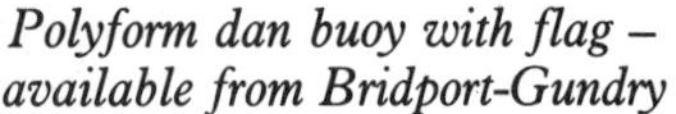

Polyform dan buoy with flag – available from Bridport-Gundry

Polyform dan buoy with radar reflector – available from Bridport-Gundry

Fishing Gear and Equipment: Klyne Fishing Co. Ltd, Battery, Greene Road, Lowestoft, Suffolk NR32 1DE.

Fishing Gear and Equipment (Scandinavian): Hugh Norman (Marine Sales) Ltd, Unit One, Castle Road, Industrial Estate, Ellon, Aberdeenshire AB4 9RF.

Fishing Journals: AGB Heighway Ltd, Cloister Court, 22–26 Farringdon Lane, London EC1R 3AU.

Floats, hard plastic: Industrial Injection Moulders Ltd, Milton Industrial Estate, Lesmahagow, Scotland ML11 0JN.

Ground Tackle (Anchors, chains, shackles etc.): Isaiah Preston Ltd, Station Street, Cradley Heath, West Midlands B64 7BA.

Line fishing tackle, lures, baits: Pegley-Davies Ltd, Hersham Trading Estate, Walton-on-Thames, Surrey KT12 3QE.

Longlining gear and deck machinery: North Sea Winches Ltd, 39/43 Roscoe Street, Scarborough, North Yorkshire YO12 7BX.

A small selection from a vast range of plastic floats marketed by Scanfloat in Norway and available in the UK from Hugh Norman

In addition to plastic floats of 14 different sizes, Industrial Injection Moulders produce net mending needles, thimbles, cod-end rings and swivels like this made of nylon

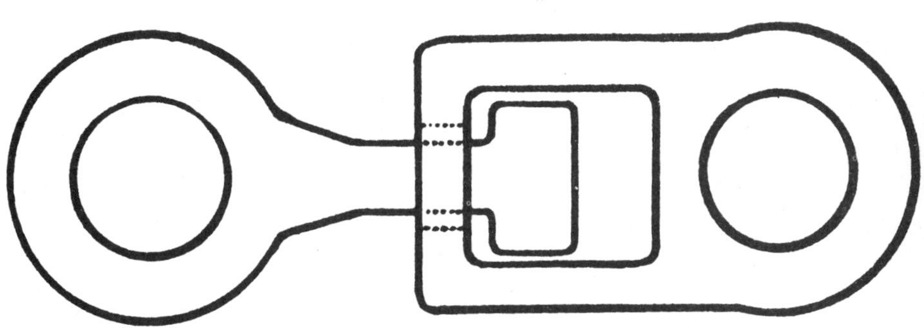

Deep sea reels, made by Asbjorn Horgard in Trondheim, are extensively used in Norway for handlining cod. They are obtainable in the UK from Pegley-Davies

Nautical Instruments: Henry Browne and Son Ltd, Sestral House, Loxford Road, Barking, Essex IG11 8PE.

Paints and antifouling compositions: Teal and Mackrill Ltd, Lockwood Street, Hull, North Humberside HU2 0HN.

Propellers and Stern Gear: Brunton's Propellers Ltd, Station Road, Sudbury, Suffolk CO10 6ST.

Pumps, manually operated bilge: Munster Simms Engineering Ltd, Old Belfast Road, Bangor, Northern Ireland BT19 1LT.

Pumps, mechanical bilge and engine cooling: Gilbert Gilkes and Gordon Ltd, Kendal, Cumbria LA9 7BZ.

Pyrotechnics and line throwers: Pains Wessex Ltd, High Post, Salisbury, Wiltshire SP4 6AS.

Radio navigation systems and instruments: Racal-Decca Marine Navigation Ltd, 87 Burlington Road, New Malden, Surrey KT3 4PD.

Radio, radar and fish finding equipment: The Marconi International Marine Co. Ltd, Elettra House, Westway, Chelmsford, Essex CM1 3BH.

Radar and fish finders: Racal-Decca Marine Radar Ltd, Burlington House, Burlington Road, New Malden, Surrey KT3 4NW.

Ropes, fibre and wire: British Ropes Ltd, Carr Hill, Doncaster, South Yorkshire DN4 8DG.

Ropes, wire: John Shaw Ltd, Sandy Lane, Worksop, Nottinghamshire S80 3ES. Depots in London and Aberdeen.

Gilkes pumps are durable, reliable and extensively used in fishing vessels

R. & B. Leakey specialise to a considerable extent in making folding traps like this one for capturing prawns, lobsters and crabs

Shellfish Traps (Folding): R. & B. Leakey, The Sutcliffe House, Settle, North Yorkshire BD24 0BA.

Ship's Chandlers: Thomas Foulke, 3(JB) Sansome Road, Leytonstone, London E11 3HB.

Vibration and noise suppressors: Halyard Marine Ltd, 2 Portsmouth Centre, Quartermain's Road, Old Airport, Portsmouth, Hampshire PO3 5QT.

Wheelhouse window wipers: Wynstruments Ltd, Staverton Airport, Gloucester GL2 9QU.

Wood preservatives: Cuprinol Ltd, Adderwell, Frome, Somerset BA11 1NL.

Glossary

Armouring	the large-meshed outer walls of a trammel net
Bar	one side of a mesh
Bating	the process of reducing the number of meshes by taking into one mesh two meshes of the preceding row
Bating Piece	the section of a trawl between the square and the upper section of the cod-end
Beam Trawl	a conical net with the upper side of its mouth fitted to a wood or iron beam and iron heads or shoes which keep the beam off the seabed
Bellies	two pieces of netting, usually tapered along each side, joined together along the sides. The bellies form the body of a trawl; they are joined between the square and the lengtheners
Braid	to make a net by hand
Braided (cordage)	plaited ropes or lines in which the yarns or filaments cross one another nearly at right angles
Bridle	length of rope about twice the length of the beam shackled at either end to the forward ends of a beam trawl's heads
Buff	a large, inflated pear-shaped buoy used for floating and marking the position of nets; formerly made of canvas but now invariably made of brightly coloured plastic material.
Cast	a line between two and five metres long, fitted between a main handline and its sinker to which baited hooks and lures are attached by droppers
Clips	devices made of metal, designed for attaching snoods to longlines without using knots
Cod-end	the tail of a trawl which holds the fish. It is usually made from double mesh netting and consists of two pieces of netting which are straight along the sides

Cod-line	small, three-stranded line usually made of hemp; thin rope of high breaking strength threaded through the meshes at the extremity of a cod-end to close it
Cod Ripping Gear	arrangement of hooks, lures and sinkers used to catch cod in Scottish waters
Coil	usually a 220 metre length of rope
Cork line	line with small corks or floats attached to it from which gill and tangle nets are suspended
Creeper	device used to recover lines, traps or nets lost on the seabed
Creel	lobster or crab trap with one or two entrances through the sides
Dan (Dhan) Buoy	marker buoy pierced by a staff with a flag or light at the top and a weight at the bottom to keep it vertical in the water
Demersal (fish)	fish which feed on or near the seabed
Drift Net	net suspended vertically in the water, free to drift with the current and trap specific species of fish by the gills
Dory	small, double-ended, flat-bottomed, open boat originally developed for hand-lining cod off the Atlantic coast of North America
Drifter	a vessel used mainly for working drift nets
Dropper	short length of line, usually made of monofilament nylon, used for attaching a hook to a cast
Float line	same as Cork line
Gaff	strong wooden staff with large unbarbed hook fitted at one end, used for lifting heavy fish inboard
Gill Net	net with mesh of a particular size designed to trap specific species of fish by the gills
Greeper	device used to recover lines, traps or nets lost on the seabed
Groundrope	length of fibre rope with weights on it, or wire rope with rubber discs or bobbins on it, to which the forward bottom end of a trawl is attached
Handline	line with one or more baited hooks attached at the lower end
Headline	strong fibre or combination rope attached to square and top wings of a trawl
Heads	iron fittings at either end of a trawl's beam which keep it off the seabed

Hooks	ringed – those with a ring at one end for attaching dropper or snood flatted – those with a flattened end to the shank spade – same as flatted tinned – those treated with metallic coating to prevent them rusting
Hoop Net	device comprised of an iron hoop with a conically-shaped piece of netting attached to it; used for catching lobsters, prawns and flat fish
Inner (wall)	small mesh wall of netting rigged between the two large mesh outer walls of a trammel net
Jig (to)	to lower and raise baited hooks and sinker to and from the seabed repeatedly
Lask	piece of silver-coloured skin cut from a mackerel or other fish for use as bait
Leaded line	line with pieces of lead attached to it at intervals; used to sink gill and tangle nets
Leadline	line with continuous lead core, used to sink gill and tangle nets; light line with 2–4 kg lead at the lower end for measuring depth and ascertaining the nature of the seabed
Line, Monofilament	line made from a single continuous filament of nylon large enough to be used on its own
Line, Multifilament	line made from strands of continuous filaments too small to be used on their own, twisted together
Line, Staple Spun	lines made from filaments which have been cut into short lengths and then spun into yarns prior to being twisted into strands and then into lines
Linnet, Lint	small-meshed central wall of a trammel net
Longline	line with hooks attached by snoods at intervals
Lure	artificial bait made of feathers, metal, rubber or plastic materials
Mesh	fabric of twine with four sides or bars of equal length
Mesh, full	the distance between the centre of one knot and the centre of the next diagonally opposite knot
Mesh, inside	the measurement from the inside of one knot to the inside of the next diagonally opposite knot
Mesh, stretched	the longer measurement along the side of a sheet of netting when all meshes are closed

Meshes, clean	meshes along the edges of a piece of netting with knots which, when untied, leave an intact mesh or loop of twine
Meshes, cut	meshes along the edges of a piece of netting with knots that cannot be untied without breaking down the mesh
Nobby	fishing smack of unique design used on the coast of Lancashire
Outer (wall)	one of the large mesh walls rigged on either side of the small mesh inner wall (lint) of a trammel net
Outrigger	long, slender pole which can be slung outboard by means of a tackle at the masthead to tow extra trolling lines wide of the wake of a boat
Paravane	device used for shearing – often used for shearing trolled lures to either side of a boat or into deep water astern of one
Parlour Pot	lobster or crab trap with two compartments, one of which has entrances through both sides and the other a single entrance from the first; the first contains the bait and from the second escape is practically impossible
Pelagic (fish)	fish which do not feed on the seabed
Pockets	arrangements of netting on the inner side of a trawl which taper towards the mouth and so prevent fish escaping
Pot	shellfish trap with single entrance through top
Railing	trolling for mackerel
Riddle	round sieve with parallel wires fitted across the bottom; used for sorting shrimps
Shoes	iron fittings at either end of a trawl's beam which keep it off the seabed
Shoot	to stream nets or longlines over the stern of a boat
Snood	length of monofilment, twisted or braided line used for attaching hooks to longlines
Sole Rope	fibre rope fitted along the bottom of a gill or tangle net
Stand	wooden spar, weighted at the bottom end, used to spread the end of a trammel net and keep it vertical in the water
Tangle Net	net such as a trammel in which fish become entangled instead of being caught by the gills

Tickler Chain	length of chain wound around the groundrope of a trawl, or shackled between the heads of a beam trawl, to increase catches of flat fish
Trace	line, usually made of monofilament nylon, secured to the lower end of a main handline, to which baits or lures are attached by droppers
Trammel Net	tangle net with three parallel walls of different sized mesh
Troll	to tow lures astern of a boat to catch pelagic fish
Whiffling	trolling for mackerel